BASIL
MOREAU

Gary MacEoin's biography of Fr. Moreau appears at a most appropriate time, when many, even many of us who know Fr. Moreau, want to learn more about his life and contribution to the church and society. MacEoin's gentle and respectful style brings Fr. Moreau to life in a way few others of his biographers have, and I hope this new edition receives wide reading.

Father John Jenkins, C.S.C.
President, the University of Notre Dame

Gary MacEoin's fine work captures the painful reality of the cross in Basil Moreau's life. The book also poignantly portrays Moreau's ability to embrace the cross as the gift of hope so central to the mission of his fledgling Congregation.

Father David Tyson, C.S.C.
Provincial Superior, Indiana Province of the Congregation of Holy Cross

Through his bold attention to both the dark and light facts of Basil Moreau's life, Gary MacEoin illuminates the virtues of zeal, humility, and forgiveness that guided Moreau's life, virtues that will challenge every reader.

Sister Joy O'Grady, C.S.C.
President of Sisters of the Holy Cross

A progressive educator who aimed to revitalize religion through wider diffusion of knowledge, Moreau was committed to the excellent professional preparation of Holy Cross faculty. That commitment has born excellent fruit. Everyone in Holy Cross ministry should read this book.

Carol Ann Mooney, Ph.D.
President, Saint Mary's College

Father Moreau's story is one of hope in turbulent times, one that still inspires us to be faithful to our call in spite of difficulties and obstacles. The Holy Cross tradition he founded continues to benefit the world, and his vision for teaching young people is as stimulating today as it was then.

George E. Martin, Ph.D.
President, St. Edward's University

MacEoin's biography of Basil Moreau is a reminder of how the cross was woven into the whole cloth which was the founder's life. This story as told by MacEoin is more than history; it is sustenance for our continuing journey from faith to hope, and well worth reading again.

Richard B. Gilman, C.S.C.
President, Holy Cross College

BASIL MOREAU

Founder of HOLY CROSS

GARY MacEOIN
Revised and Updated by Joel Giallanza, C.S.C.

Foreword by Hugh Cleary, C.S.C.
Superior General of the Congregation of Holy Cross

ave maria press AmP notre dame, indiana

Nihil Obstat:
John F. Murphy, S.T.D.
Censor librorum

Imprimatur:
William E. Cousins
Archbishop of Milwaukee
March 13, 1962

Founded in 1865, Ave Maria Press is a ministry of the Indiana Province of Holy Cross.

www.avemariapress.com

ISBN-10 1-59471-133-X   ISBN-13 978-1-59471-133-6

Cover and text design by John Carson

Photographs provided by Brother George Klawitter, C.S.C.

Printed and bound in the United States of America.

Cataloging-in-Publication Data is available from the Library of Congress.

Contents

Foreword

I n the closing chapter of his sympathetic and appreciative 1962 biography of Father Basil Moreau, Gary MacEoin leaves off eagerly anticipating the conclusion of the second stage of the canonization process for the long-suffering founder of the Congregation of Holy Cross.

In 1955 the Cause of Father Moreau had been formally opened; by 1957 he was declared "Servant of God," the first of four stages leading to canonization. On May 10, 1961, the Promoter of the Faith for the Cause submitted to the Congregation of Rites within the Vatican Curia the required supporting documents testifying to Father Moreau's heroic virtues, which would award him the title Venerable. All was progressing well. It is clear that MacEoin awaited a positive decision.

However a year later, on October 11, 1962, Pope John XXIII convened the Second Vatican Council initiating a period of unprecedented change within the Catholic Church and thereby within the Congregation of Holy Cross. All levels of ecclesial life, including religious communities, experienced dramatic shifts in priorities as the vision of the Council was implemented. Religious congregations were urged to renew themselves in accord with the founding charism of their respective orders.

The Congregation of Holy Cross embraced the Council's called-for period of experimentation with great enthusiasm. In the process, attention shifted away from pursuing the formalities of

Father Moreau's Cause in favor of undertaking a vibrant renewal within the founding charism.

With the Vatican Council's emphasis on liturgical renewal Pope Paul VI, in 1969, divided the Congregation of Rites into two separate entities: the Congregation for Divine Worship and the Congregation for the Causes of Saints. The agenda for liturgical renewal was immense; the agenda for the Causes of Saints continued its careful yet laborious study of the relatively few causes it received.

It was not until many years later when Pope John Paul II encouraged a focused emphasis on growth in holiness among God's people that the work of the Congregation for the Causes of Saints assumed greater prominence in the Church's consciousness. Following the exhortation to sanctity, the Congregation of Holy Cross once again took up the Cause of Father Moreau where it had been left off in 1961.

On April 12, 2003, the Prefect of the Vatican Congregation for the Causes of Saints promulgated, in the presence of Pope John Paul II, the decree testifying that the Servant of God Basil Moreau practiced the theological and cardinal virtues to a heroic degree. The Holy Father declared the founder of Holy Cross Venerable.

❖

Readers of McEoin's biography will find the milieu of Father Moreau's experience useful for meditation and reflection at the start of this new millennium. Many social commentators call this the postmodern age. While there are many variations to this designation, Gary MacEoin's work can help focus our attention on what is needed to live lives of unstinting hope in God's love, a love seemingly dismissed as foolish and self-defeating in a highly secular milieu.

The Congregation of Holy Cross was founded in the Age of Enlightenment, the start of the modern age. The French Revolution gave rise to a new and lasting era of de-Christianization. A

European philosophy of humanism replaced faith as the central paradigm for embodying meaning. The ideals of humanism, expressed through the French doctrine of liberty, equality, and fraternity, were actually born of Christian principles embedded in European culture, but they were not recognized as such.

Over these past two centuries these humanistic principles have slowly given way to an age of secularism. While humanism seeks the common good, secularism often serves the self, striving to amass power, wealth, and pleasure in a world of limited resources. Consumer demand for material satisfaction forges barriers between those who have and those who have not.

MacEoin's biography of Father Moreau gives us insight into the destructive web of what we might call the "social individualism" of a secular culture. We could think of this term as describing a phenomenon whereby the parts of a social system strive to become greater than the whole of that system. In striving for dominance these parts become systems unto themselves while maintaining their allegiance to the whole. Eventually the system of the common good, which had been greater than the parts, is left in ruin.

Secular ideologies tend to create division over equality, oppression over liberty, individualism over fraternity. A culture of greed is apt to dominate human consciousness. Avarice almost always employs violent strategies both to protect and amass life's temporalities.

Just as humanism can usurp faith and secularism can usurp humanism in a given culture, it is clear that these same competitive human dynamics can and do play out within the Church and religious communities, including Father Moreau's new Congregation of Holy Cross. Human beings are human beings. We are capable of great dignity and great deceit as well. Ultimately, we trust that through God's grace all things will work toward the good.

MacEoin traces the inter-relational dynamics of the key figures involved in the establishment and growth of the Congregation. It is filled with intrigue. One can almost be scandalized in reading the seemingly petty wars of will fought between the religious personalities, whether they be cardinals, bishops or religious. Even the Pope was shaken by the infighting among the religious of Holy Cross. It seemed at one moment it would be necessary for the Pope to suppress the new foundation since no intervention from the Vatican could bring a cessation to the squabbles and deceits running rampart among the members of the Congregation.

Father Moreau suffered mightily in his efforts to hold the Congregation of Holy Cross together, not as his own work but as God's. It was his hope in the cross that allowed him to suffer the torment of his soul in loving abandonment to God's Providence. His is a spirituality for our time.

❖

Father Moreau's motto for the Congregation, "The Cross, Our Only Hope," carries within it the fundamental spirituality and mission of Holy Cross.

The cross entailed in sacrificing one's self for the good of another is always difficult to carry. To live primarily for others and not for the self is a seemingly foolish approach to life and love in any age, and perhaps particularly in our own postmodern times.

The consecrated life is a gift for the human family since it is an icon of community. Our common vocation demands more than one another's forbearance; it demands self-emptying love.

Father Moreau teaches us to hope in this kind of cross. Love must endure. Embracing the cross for the sake of enduring love leads us to salvation. Pope Benedict XVI expresses simply and well the core of hope's virtue:

> Hope is practiced through the virtue of patience, which continues to do good even in the face of apparent failure, and through the virtue of humility, which accepts God's mystery and trusts him even at times of darkness (*Deus Caritas Est.*, part II, 39).

It is the hope that Father Moreau lived and the hope that will sustain us all.

❖

In celebration of Father Moreau's extraordinary life this new edition of Gary MacEoin's biography commemorates Pope Benedict XVI's April 28, 2006, promulgation of an authorized miracle attributed to the intercession of Father Moreau. This promulgation completes the beatification process. On September 15, 2007, Venerable Basile-Antoine Marie Moreau will be beatified in LeMans, France, the city where he lived and died, the home of the Congregation's Mother Church, and the sacred place where he is buried. After the Liturgy of Beatification, Father Moreau will be called Blessed, completing the third stage of the process leading to canonization.

The religious of the Congregation of Holy Cross are very grateful to Ave Maria Press for republishing this very fine and engaging biography of Father Moreau during a time of great significance. We have embarked on a year of rejoicing and renewal leading up to Venerable Moreau's beatification. We pray it will be a holy year of grace for us.

We are especially grateful that this new publication of Father Moreau's biography will not only assist Holy Cross religious in our renewal but that it will encourage and inspire our lay colleagues and collaborators in fulfilling our essential mission: bringing hope to a world so bereft of this precious gift. All who engage Father Moreau in this book will surely find inspiration to live their own lives with hope in enduring love.

Rev. Hugh Cleary, C.S.C.
Superior General
Congregation of Holy Cross
Christmas 2006

CHAPTER ONE

A Chosen Instrument

B asil Anthony Mary Moreau was one of the rare men who alter the course of history. Born into a peasant family in northwest France on February 11, 1799, he never possessed wealth or power. His path through life was strewn with failures. But he had one asset: he loved God. And that love drove him to a total utilization of vital resources such as perhaps many possess but few discover.

In his lifetime he made a major impact on France, Canada, and the United States. His zeal expressed itself in noble works in places as widely scattered as Italy, Poland, Algeria, and India. And his death began a yet more fruitful apostolate. Over a century later, his foundations still grow, spreading his spirit and achieving the aims to which his being was dedicated.

Basil Moreau's principal contribution consisted of a group of more or less closely interrelated religious communities, which he either established himself or developed from previously founded organizations. The first was the Good Shepherd convent at Le Mans—an orphanage and home for penitents, which he played a leading role in starting while a young priest of the diocese of

Le Mans, and then directed as ecclesiastical superior for twenty-one years.

Next came the Brothers of St. Joseph, a group begun by a fellow priest to teach elementary schools and handed over to him by the founder who recognized that his age and circumstances were handicapping the growth of an organization for which a desperate need existed. The third step was an association of Auxiliary Priests to act as superiors for the Brothers, give missions in the diocese, and teach secondary schools.

The Brothers and priests were gradually transformed into the Congregation of Holy Cross, and in the process yet another congregation of women was established, first as a part of Holy Cross and with the initial purpose of housekeeping for the men, later as a separate organization with a broad teaching and nursing function of its own. As it developed, it broke into three administratively separate units, one in France, one in Canada, and one in the United States.

Basil Moreau's genius was that he could get people to come together and pool their efforts to accomplish the purposes he proposed. The drama of his life is to be found on his desk, from which went forth year after year proposals, plans, and projects to capture the imagination and win new helpers as well as to retain the interest of those already committed. But he had not only to create, he had also to finance. And here again we see his organizing techniques, expressed in the broad-based Associations of the Good Shepherd and of St. Joseph, which enlisted the continuing support of thousands of lay people.

His life is, accordingly, less a chronology of personal incidents than the story of the development of his works. When conflict develops, it is not so much the clash of right and wrong or good and evil as that of good people differing honestly as regards the best way to reach the goal on which all are agreed. The work is endangered not through an innate weakness but through an excess of vitality, which impels it beyond its capabilities.

The more I reflect on Basil Moreau, the more I liken him to Ignatius of Loyola. It would be hard to think of two men of God farther apart in their human characteristics than the Spanish nobleman and the French peasant, differences which were projected in the formal discipline of Loyola's Society of Jesus and the atmosphere of relaxed spontaneity which the visitor observes in communities of Moreau's Congregation of Holy Cross. There is, nevertheless, a basic similarity in their analysis of the world circumstances which led each to found a religious order.

Ignatius at thirty in the year 1521 resolved on a total dedication to God. Prayer, meditation, study, and earnest search for the divine will led to the foundation of the Society of Jesus thirteen years later. He saw the Church threatened through deep-seated internal corruption and fossilization of institutions, and challenged in a death struggle by the formidable external foe of Protestantism.

Basil Moreau made his total dedication somewhat earlier in life than Ignatius. One cannot fix a precise date, but most probably he took the crucial decision while a seminarian, perhaps no more than twenty. A longer interval separated him from the logical goal of his reasoning and action. It was harder for him than for Ignatius—a soldier and member of the ruling class—to see himself in the role of founder. But the facts drove him inescapably. The Church in France was in crisis. Gallicanism had for two centuries restricted the arteries through which flowed its lifeblood from the heart of Christendom. The Revolution had cut off its sources of material and intellectual nourishment by seizing its property and closing its schools, and the prophets of the Age of Reason were plausibly announcing the proximate interment of the corpse.

Sometimes one is tempted to wonder why a founder starts a new religious order rather than draft one already dedicated to the aims he seeks. In this case, the reason is clear: Religious orders had been stamped out in France by the Revolution. Those that survived underground or precariously re-established themselves lacked legal status. Not only were they harassed by the civil administration, but even some bishops were strongly opposed to the creation or restoration of organizations entitled to canonical exemption from diocesan control.

France was thus a country where everything had to be begun anew, from catechism teaching in the villages to the conquest of scholastic freedom, from the hasty recruiting of a depleted clergy to the re-establishment of the religious life under varied forms, from the apostolate to the masses by means of missions and retreats to the methodical introduction of well-organized studies in colleges and seminaries.

Basil Moreau was inspired to take a big part in all of this. He did not seek the role of founder. What he was conscious of was needs, a broad spectrum of needs affecting every aspect of society, but particularly a need for educators to form Christian minds and hearts, and of priests to preach the Gospel and administer the sacraments.

To meet these needs, he created instruments, each of which had to have two characteristics. They had to be able to perform the required function. And they had to be capable of existing within the legal and political environment. The logic of events did the rest. It pushed them gradually into the pattern in which the religious life had traditionally flourished in the Church. Few founders have left so many religious families, and yet Basil Moreau can to a considerable extent be called a founder by accident.

This, however, is far from suggesting that his work lacked a purpose and personality. The purposes of the Congregation of Holy Cross are described in the Constitutions in terms, which permit a very broad range of work, and historically the members have been and are involved in activities so disparate as not to fit in any neat category. Yet such universality of purpose makes perfect sense in the context of their origin. Basil's idea was the same as that of Ignatius, who in 1538 brought his first six companions to Rome to place them at the Pope's disposal. His purpose was as wide as the needs of the Church.

Like Ignatius, too, he was acutely conscious that it belonged to the Pope to determine which needs deserved priority. Obedience to Rome was one of his most developed characteristics, and many of his trials were to stem from his determined defense of papal rights.

The purpose of the Congregation of Holy Cross is similar to that of the Society of Jesus, but the personality or spirit of the two orders is very different. Ignatius thought of social groupings in terms of the army, a strong esprit de corps supported by a strict discipline. Basil Moreau took the family as his model, and the strengths and weaknesses of his organization were those of a family bound more by common aspirations, common experience, mutual affection, and sharing of sufferings than by the cold words of a contract.

It has been my privilege to intimately know members of many religious orders and to observe from the inside the workings of not a few communities. But never have I had such a sense of family as in the mother house of Holy Cross. The relationship of the religious to each other, to their superior, and to the wider grouping of the laity who attend their church mirrored the informality, the affection, and the sense of common ends unselfishly pursued which one hopes characterize one's own family.

The Benedictines have something of this, but the stress seems to be greater in Holy Cross. That the founder was responsible for this spirit, no one who has studied his life and read his letters to his spiritual children can ever doubt.

To note just one aspect, Father Moreau in an early circular described his plan for a family or a community of three societies of priests, Brothers, and Sisters dedicated not merely to Jesus, Mary, and Joseph, but to the hearts of Jesus, Mary, and Joseph. The heart is the symbol of love, and love is the bond of union. As Father Thomas Barrosse, C.S.C., stresses in a study of Holy Cross spirituality, Father Moreau did not propose these hearts as objects of special devotion but rather as symbols of the union of love which he wished to keep vividly in the thoughts of his religious.

The early seal of the Congregation consisted of an anchor entwined by a banner bearing the initials of Jesus, Mary, and Joseph and surmounted by three hearts. To some, the symbolism may smack of a sentimentality we associate with plaster saints and overcommercialized religious art, but one must recognize it as a valid communications technique in nineteenth-century France. Its basic soundness is evidenced by its success in infusing into the members of the Congregation a spirit that made them consciously model their mutual relations on those of the Holy Family. To that end, Father Moreau called his priests "Salvatorists," his Sisters "Marianites," and his Brothers "Josephites" after their models, Jesus, Mary, and Joseph.

Of course the Holy Family started with an important advantage. Not all members of Father Moreau's family were saints. Some understood but poorly the obligations they had assumed. Family differences led to family estrangements, to challenges against parental authority. Father Moreau was crushed precisely as a father. Many of his children rejected him.

Children can be very cruel, and Holy Cross was cruel to its father. But it sinned the way a family does, and in due course it made amends as a family does. An estrangement seldom breaks family ties. The family remains so long as there is a sense of common purpose, of shared experiences, of affection transcending legal obligation. The more real these elements, the more violent the clash, but also the more certain the reconciliation—and, needless to add, the tighter the resulting family bonds.

If, as was suggested, the family looms large in Father Moreau's view of social organization, this attitude was the result of no accident. He came from a long line of French peasants whose community had the characteristics of a widespread family and whose lives were ruled by personal loyalties and obligations deriving ultimately from a sense of membership in a family group. From this lived and shared experience, he could draw countless examples to demonstrate that such an organization of life was suited to bring out the best qualities in a man.

A fugitive priest with a price on his head baptized him. He grew up among memories and living examples of those who had succumbed to persecution and those who had withstood. The pastor who taught him catechism, reading, writing, arithmetic, and Latin had secretly exercised his ministry throughout the Reign of Terror. Such memories would make Basil regard heroicity as almost normal.

He was fortunate in his parents, too. In a time of war and separation, they lived together and at peace. His father was drafted neither into the Vendean armies, which vainly sought to defend religion against the new irreligion, nor into the legions, which carried the Emperor's ambition into a score of conquered capitals and finally buried it under the snowdrifts of a Russian winter. Both Louis and Louise Moreau gave their children the example of a Christian life and trained them in the natural virtues, which form the substratum of supernatural holiness.

This is not an uncommon background. Rather it is the traditional social context in which vocations to the priesthood and to the religious life develop. Additional factors must be isolated if we are to offer a logical explanation of why Basil Moreau not only became a priest and a religious but dedicated all his energies throughout his life to the single purpose of promoting the Kingdom of God.

One fairly constant natural characteristic of the saints is a strong personality. This may to some extent be a result as well as a cause of their holiness. A man totally dedicated to God's service will not let anything stand in his way if satisfied that a course of action is God's will. But strong natural qualities usually precede holiness in those who become saints, and Basil Moreau seems to have been endowed with such qualities.

A strong will and an ardent temperament, however, make a two-edged weapon. Under the influence of grace, they urge the person who possesses them to devote himself unreservedly to

the service of God. But almost immediately they begin to constitute an obstacle to the execution of this purpose, since the
candidate for perfection must learn to divest himself of his own
will and curb his impetuosities.

All this occurred in the early stages of Basil Moreau's efforts to
acquire holiness. The period of graduate study spent at the seminary of St. Sulpice, Paris, immediately after his ordination, played
no less decisive a part in his spiritual than in his intellectual formation. It is ironic that he himself was grievously disappointed
at the decision to send him to St. Sulpice and that the man who
singled him out for special training was later as bishop to test
severely the virtue there acquired.

The first thing St. Sulpice did was place him in a stimulating
intellectual atmosphere. The academic preparation of candidates
for the priesthood in France was then far below what would
today be an acceptable minimum. The Revolution had disrupted
the seminary system and decimated the clergy. Priests were desperately needed for pastoral work, and few qualified professors
were available. To complicate the situation, the theology taught
in the seminaries was usually infected with the historically allied
heresies of Jansenism and Gallicanism.*

These heresies were not without influence on Basil's life, but
for the moment it suffices to say that as a seminarian he seems to
have shied instinctively away from them. It was important, however, that he should acquire a theoretical justification for what he
felt to be right, and such grounding in theology was supplied at
St. Sulpice, where he was fortunate enough to build for himself
a defense against Gallicanism without following Lamennais into
the contrary error at the other end of the intellectual spectrum.

---

*Jansenism was the popular religious movement of the seventeenth and
eighteenth centuries begun by theologian Cornelius Otto Jansen and
characterized by extreme personal piety and a belief in predestination.
Gallicanism was the religious philosophy popular in France beginning in
the seventeenth century, which sought to curtail papal authority by defin-
ing it in a much narrower way by granting more importance to bishops
and civil leaders.

Still more decisive was the spiritual formation given him by St. Sulpice. For the first time he felt the influence of a school of piety in the strict sense of the term. Sulpician piety, derived from Father Olier, founder of the Sulpicians, has two major character- istics—a purgative element of severe mortification and a unitive element of adherence to Christ and participation in his mysteries. Mortification was already present in Father Moreau's life. What he needed was a counterbalance to prevent development of a self- centered and stultifying masochism.

It is not easy to put the penances of the saints in proper per- spective. To begin paradoxically, one might say that deliberate acts of self-punishment characterize every saint yet are of their nature only remotely related to sanctity. Most people are terri- fied of physical pain, though it is no harder to train the body to endure physical punishment than to acquire a new intellectual discipline, like learning a language. Neither grace nor supernatu- ral intention is any more a necessary prerequisite in the one case than in the other. History presents many examples of this, from the warrior classes of pre-Discovery Mexico to the firewalkers of modern India.

Father Moreau's personal regime of penance and self-sacrifice frightens the imagination unless placed in perspective. He scourged himself and wore metal girdles with sharp points that dug into the skin at each movement. His instruments of penance can now be inspected at Sainte-Croix and Notre Dame. I do not want to discount this self-conquest, but I do insist that it can be achieved in a few months and will subsequently prove no more irksome than the appliances many wear happily to ease a physi- cal defect or discomfort.

I am somewhat more impressed by Father Moreau's abstemi- ousness and still more by the rigor with which he limited his sleeping hours. In the middle of his active life, he stopped going to bed altogether, and for his last twenty-five years he slept sit- ting in a deep armchair, at least in part because of an accident that damaged his leg, a practice abandoned only on the doctor's insistence a few days before his death.

By themselves, nevertheless, these things would not prove much. Comparable self-control is a matter of daily observation on the part not only of persons suffering from certain illnesses, such as diabetes, but also on that of thousands of people with no higher motive than to stay slim.

What such disciplines demonstrate for me is the presence of a strong motivation, of a decision by a determined man to gain complete mastery over his body in order to use it with maximum efficiency for the ulterior end. To achieve notable success in any order, a man must learn to drive himself. The successful business executive works a seventy-hour week to win the wealth and power he covets. What self-denial demonstrates in the case of one who seeks holiness is that he is serious enough in his quest to take the first preparatory step.

Immediately, however, a temptation arises to identify the means with the end, to measure progress in holiness by the intensity of the self-discipline achieved. A remarkable priest who took charge of him at St. Sulpice helped Father Moreau over this hurdle. He was Father Mollevaut, superior at the Solitude of Issy, a man who combined personal spirituality with an understanding of human nature. The Solitude, an annex to which Father Moreau transferred from the main college in his second year, lived up to its name. The students followed a routine similar to that of a novitiate, removed from outside distractions, with long hours of silence, and with much of their time devoted to meditation and spiritual exercises.

Father Moreau brought with him such habits of self-restraint. His boyhood had been spent in a home in which poverty was normal and each member trained to make his or her contribution. Social attitudes reflected the rigid Jansenistic code common in France at the time. The priests he knew best had abandoned their comforts, risked their lives, engaged in menial works, endured prison.

As a student, after receiving minor orders and with his spiritual director's approval, he anticipated by a private vow the celibacy to be imposed with the subdiaconate. He bound himself to an obedience which would accept all assignments and seek none and to a poverty which would accumulate no riches and wear only unostentatious dress. He pledged himself to fast on Fridays and in the seminary to drink only water at the collation on fast days.

Father Mollevaut did not take long to recognize the quality and characteristics of the material with which he was working. Here was a man progressing toward holiness by using the very formula prescribed by the Sulpician school of spirituality. He was conscious of the danger of an excessive development of the purgative element of penance, and he moved to balance and humanize it by an attitude of adherence to Christ and participation in His mysteries.

Simultaneously, he counseled moderation in public acts of mortification, which might create a reputation as an ascetic and encourage spiritual pride. His success may be judged by the fact that, while Father Moreau always observed self-denial, he gave his religious families a comparatively mild rule on mortification. He set before them an ideal as high as his practice, to deny themselves in everything they could do without, but the specific restrictions and prescribed acts of penance he made less demanding than those of many other religious orders.

Another problem with which Father Mollevaut dealt firmly was Father Moreau's tendency to be carried away by his enthusiasms. When he looked at the extreme shortage of priests in rural France, he wanted to take charge of a country parish. When he meditated on the lives of the Fathers of the Desert, he felt impelled to become a Trappist. Reading about the vast lands still in the darkness of paganism, he believed he heard God call him to the foreign missions.

For such impetuosity Father Mollevaut had a simple antidote. God has called you to your present functions, he would say, and you must continue them until obedience orders you elsewhere. He had to repeat this counsel many times over the years, for Father Moreau was continually haunted by the vision of all the good works that were crying out to be done. It seems obvious that Father Mollevaut was not formulating an absolute rule of conduct. He was concerned with a particular case, and his judgment told him that Father Moreau needed a longer period of training and of instruction in piety before he could launch out on the original works to which he was being called.

If Father Mollevaut's direction succeeded in injecting a supernatural element into Father Moreau's actions, it did so without altering his natural attitudes. Among the reproaches later lodged against him by those who clashed with him over his administration as head of the Congregation of Holy Cross, there are frequent references to a violent temper. He himself did not challenge such criticisms. "I recognize my faults of this kind," he once wrote with disarming frankness to a colleague, who apparently had reported to him that Bishop Bouvier of Le Mans was complaining of his temper. However, he immediately added a justification which is admirable for its objectivity. "But at the same time, without this 'temper,' is it not true that Sainte-Croix would have been wiped out of existence the day the Bishop told me at the bottom of the stairs in his house: 'If you teach Latin, I will never again set foot inside Sainte-Croix'? This temper has stood firm against all his opposition, just as it also resisted his theological teaching. Is there anything wrong with that?"

What Father Mollevaut sought, and what he achieved, was simply to establish control over his natural impulses so that he could channel them to good ends. It is noteworthy that in all his correspondence, even in reply to the most insulting and provoking charges, Father Moreau's words are always tempered with patience and affection. This all followed from the pattern of Father Mollevaut's direction, which sought principally to encourage his pupil to model his life on that of Christ and acquire through meditation on the mysteries of Christ's life a deeper understanding of the plan of redemption and his own part in it. A gradual transformation of the man thus took place, an emptying out of his defects and selfish impulses, a substitution of the attitudes, motives, and purposes of Christ.

The final result was an ability to view events through Christ's eyes and to react to them with Christ's reaction. The intention of Sulpician piety is to saturate the man in Christ, to familiarize him so completely with the incidents of Christ's life and His method of dealing with them that he reaches the point of thinking and doing as Christ would have thought and done in like circumstances.

Such a regime produces a complicated and well-rounded man. It is certainly far removed from negative and do-nothing acceptance of the divine plan, which is what some people erroneously consider holiness. The value of this kind of training was to be demonstrated in Father Moreau's life, since less could hardly have carried him unscathed through the trials he endured. For, like Christ, he would be betrayed and rejected by his own.

CHAPTER TWO

Youth in Revolutionary France

The ninth of fourteen children, Basil Moreau was early habituated to poverty, discipline, and work. He had to be active and resourceful, to put his hand to practical affairs, to do things for himself, to give much and expect little.

The Christian virtues were stressed. Basil's nephew and first biographer described his uncle's boyhood home: "Fear of God, love of the Church, prayer in common, a laborious life, filial obedience, respect for authority—these were, for Louis Moreau and his virtuous wife, family traditions which they strove to pass on to their children as the most important part of the family heritage."

The village of Laigné-en-Belin had been caught up in the religious persecution that constituted an integral part of the Reign of Terror in the first years of the Revolution. The pastor died under house arrest, and his assistant went into exile. Other priests, risking their lives, administered the sacraments in the homes of the people. Basil often recalled that one of these had baptized him, and he heard many a vivid story of their bravery and spirit of sacrifice.

The village school, which had functioned in Laigné before the Revolution, had, like most schools in France, been operated by the Church. It had been seized at the same time as other Church property, and for years not a single child in the village was taught to read and write. When Basil was nine, however, Church-State tension had eased considerably, and the pastor could assemble some of the brighter children in the rectory for informal classes, whenever he found time to teach them.

Basil soon struck the pastor as a boy who might make a good priest. When he spoke to the parents, they didn't know what to say. Nothing could please them more, but who would pay for higher education? And if the project collapsed when the time came for college, the boy would be at a dead end.

A compromise was reached. He might study, so long as he carried his share of the farm chores to prepare for what would be his life if things went wrong. He therefore drove the cows each day to pasture, carrying with him note pads and books, and a wooden box on which to write his assignments.

The pastor, Father Le Provost, was one of those determined priests who had braved the Terror. When he wanted something, he got it. And in due course, he found a way to pay for Basil's advanced education. The identity of the benefactor is uncertain, but it most probably was the lady who taught the girls while he himself looked after the boys.

In 1814, consequently, a few months after Napoleon's exile to Elba, Basil set off for high school at Chateau-Gontier, sixty miles away. His father walked with the fifteen-year-old that first day, helping to carry the few belongings and making the arrangements with the principal. Then he turned around and walked home again.

A detail like this about the father is an anticipation and explanation of the son who packed into his lifetime the achievements of a hundred other people, who founded and directed religious institutes, establishing communities on four continents, who raised and spent millions of dollars for education and pious works without ever having any secure source of income, who wrote important works of pedagogy and spirituality, who continued into his seventies to travel from parish to parish as a missionary.

In such characteristics, Basil Moreau reflected his background and the traditions of the Province of Le Maine in which his family had deep roots. The people of this part of northwest France, midway between Paris and the Breton coast, are known for their restrained character and their simple and honest way of life. They do not always contradict their opponents face to face, nor do they yield a point too easily. They are more realists than idealists, less given to lawsuits than their neighbors in Normandy, but nonetheless insistent on their rights.

Boarding school did not change the atmosphere. Rather, it intensified the influences of Basil's home and native village. The principal was Father Horeau, a man with a unique record as a fighter for religion and education. He had been thrown in prison with the entire faculty a few years before Basil was born. The pupils were disbanded and the six hundred year-old school converted into stables, an army warehouse, and finally a jail.

But Father Horeau survived the storm. Once released, he began to reorganize. The school soon flourished again, notwithstanding official resistance to independent educational activities, a resistance that become open antagonism when forty students joined an insurgent army operating in nearby Brittany and La Vendée.

Here Basil thrived and expanded. Back home he had the reputation of a leader who "got games organized and kept everything going," as a companion later reported. Father Horeau took to him from the start, soon naming him a prefect and picking him to help the overworked staff by teaching a junior class. He performed so competently that some years later Father Horeau recommended him for the posts of philosophy professor and school principal.

Here, too, Basil met another priest who would guide him for several critical years while he felt his way toward his life's vocation, who intervened in many of his critical decisions, and who finally died in the mother house of Holy Cross. Father Louis Jean

Fillion, the assistant director, was responsible for the spiritual development of the students. Although he was eleven years older than Basil, the two developed a close friendship marked by that mutual confidence and respect that come from the opening of one soul to another.

Two years completed Basil's secondary school course, two years on top of six spent in part-time primary schooling. It was a narrow foundation on which to start higher studies, and yet he was more advanced than most of his companions. Such was the level to which education had fallen in France in the first quarter of the nineteenth century.

The problem, like most of those with which Basil would be concerned throughout his life, went back to the French Revolution. Before that time, the country had had an elaborate network of schools, nearly all of them operated by the Church. The diocese of Le Mans alone had more than 320 schools for 274 communes.

Within a few years of the proclamation of the Rights of Man, all of this had been wiped out. Few of the revolutionaries had set out with the idea of persecuting the Church, any more than they had intended to destroy the monarchy. But the forces released in the midst of violence developed their own logic and produced results nobody had anticipated.

For budgetary no less than ideological reasons, it was decided to seize the property of the Church, subject to an obligation on the part of the State to pay for the maintenance of the church buildings and of the clergy, as well as to assume the costs of the education and charitable works previously carried on by the Church.

Very soon, however, the State decided that, since it was now paying for education, it had the right to establish control over its content and, specifically, to substitute the revolutionary slogans for the catechism. Then, in 1790 and the following years, the religious congregations were dispersed and their schools closed. The process was completed by a decision that the clergy at all levels should be elected by the citizens, instead of being named by the king or by their superiors, a step which created a state-controlled church structure, recognition of which meant schism. Priests and teachers who refused to take the 'constitutional' oath, as the formula pledging acceptance of the new regime for the Church came to be called, were ejected from their rectories and schools. Pius VI, for his part, declared the provision "sacrilegious, schismatic, destructive of the rights of the primacy of our see and those of the Church."

Efforts were made to keep the schools open, but local authorities were seldom able to find qualified teachers. Usually they had to depend on priests who had taken the oath and were consequently distrusted by the people, or on adventurers and incompetents. In desperation, the authorities lowered qualifications so that a teacher was recognized and paid a salary, varying with the number of pupils he could assemble, provided he could present a certificate of patriotism and of good conduct. Ideological content continued, nevertheless, to be stressed. An edict required that anyone teaching principles or maxims contrary to the laws or morality of the republic was to be denounced and punished, and soon the national assembly assumed the function of editing textbooks. In all this conflict and confusion, practically no primary schools operated anywhere for ten years, so that an entire segment of the population grew to adulthood without schooling.

The climate improved with Napoleon's rise to power in 1799. He knew that lasting internal peace required a reconciliation with the Church. Not only did the masses retain a nostalgic attachment to their religious heritage, but many intellectuals had reacted against the excesses of the revolutionary period. The thesis that the attacks on religion had been the cause of all the current social evils was gaining ground, and many were thinking about the Church in the terms in which Chateaubriand expressed himself a little later: "The modern world owes everything to it, from agriculture to the abstract sciences, from hospitals for the unfortunate to the temples built by Michelangelo and decorated by Raphael."

The result was the Concordat of 1801. The Pope succeeded in getting France to rescind the most objectionable features of the civil constitution of the clergy. But he had to make great concessions. Bishops would continue to be named by the Government, and the confiscation of all Church property was accepted as a fact. Ecclesiastics would instead receive salaries, a concession that was simultaneously a gain for the State, since it gave it a powerful weapon with which to exercise control over the clergy. In addition, only the secular clergy was granted recognition, the monastic orders—all of which had been suppressed—being passed over in silence. And finally, no act of the Holy See could be published in France without government approval.

Religious life, nevertheless, began to revive rapidly, although still subjected to many difficulties. Wars continued to gobble up revenue, leaving nothing for education. In the cities, where the well-to-do could pay tuition, schools began to appear. But the countryside continued to be neglected. The situation in Laigné-en-Belin, which remained entirely without education until the pastor started his informal classes when Basil Moreau was nine, was typical. And even where a school functioned, the level of instruction tended to be very low, since facilities for the training or recruitment of teachers did not exist. For a long time the custom continued of men and women teachers going from village to village, sporting one feather in their cap if able to teach reading, two if writing, and three if also arithmetic.

In such circumstances, bishops had to be satisfied with a minimum of preparation on the part of candidates for admission to the major seminary. France was desperate for priests. Nearly forty years had passed since the Revolution began. Many priests had been killed. Others had been absorbed into pastoral work in the countries which gave them refuge. Of those who took the 'constitutional' oath, some made their peace after the signing of the Concordat, but others had committed themselves so deeply that they had left or had been forced into retirement.

Because of the shortage of priests to staff them and the poverty of bishops, seminaries were slow to reopen, and young men who in happier circumstances might have heard the summons of their bishop had been swallowed up by the imperial war machine, from which their bones had been spewed across the face of Europe to rot in unhallowed ground for an unblessed cause. Between 1801 and 1815, only six thousand priests were ordained. It was estimated in the latter year that thirty thousand priests were at work in the country, nearly twenty thousand fewer than were needed. And since four-fifths of the active priests had been ordained before the Revolution, annual retirements were at a much higher than normal rate.

Le Mans had no major seminary beginning with the Revolution until 1810, when the bishop found temporary quarters in a hotel. Six years later, the students moved to St. Vincent's Abbey, a sixth-century monastery many times destroyed in wars, and for twenty-two years a military barracks. Basil was a member of the first class at St. Vincent's. By all accounts, he fit in immediately with the atmosphere of the seminary, setting an excellent example both by his moral conduct and by his intellectual progress.

The demands on his intellect were not too exacting, for the academic levels were no higher at St. Vincent's than elsewhere. To dwell on this point is not to belittle the French Church, which at that same moment was God's instrument for producing a Curé of Ars (St. John Vianney), but to stress what limited means the bishops had for rebuilding the moral ruins, and to give point to Basil Moreau's later concern for improving ecclesiastical studies.

Bailly's Manual, the theology text, was familiar to Basil from high school philosophy classes, for it attempted to combine the two sciences. It had been placed on the Index of Prohibited Books in 1792, and Basil used a revised edition.

Expurgation may have reduced error, but it did not cure the basic inadequacy of the approach, an attempted marriage of the scholastic method and the rationalism of Descartes. The argumentation was syllogistic in form but lacked the spirit and depth of the great medieval masters, scarcely mentioning St. Thomas Aquinas or Suarez. A French Benedictine has well described the net effect as little more than a series of "disconnected theses, explanations left hanging in the air, lifeless objections, and pointless refutations."

Undoubtedly the parts of the course covered most thoroughly were those dealing with a series of doctrines which for long had wide support in the French Church, despite condemnation by Rome, and which were known as Gallicanism in so far as they sought to restrict the Pope's authority, and as Jansenism in so far as they laid down excessively rigorous moral rules.

No intrinsic relationship exists between these two sets of doctrines, but they both happened to develop in France about the same time and gradually became so emotionally entangled that the French clergy considered it their duty to defend rigorism as moralists and to uphold the so-called "Gallican Liberties" in dogmatic theology and in administrative matters.

The Gallican Liberties had been first set out formally by an assembly of the French bishops, under pressure from Louis XIV who was feuding with Pope Innocent XI, in 1682. They proclaimed supremacy of ecumenical councils over the Pope, a position of independence for the Church in France, and restriction of the Pope's authority to matters of faith.

Louis XIV withdrew from his extreme position some years later, after the propositions had been condemned by Pope Alexander VIII in 1690. But Gallicanism remained fashionable. The civil constitution for the clergy formulated during the French Revolution continued the Gallican attitudes. And while the Concordat of 1801 ignored the subject, Napoleon decreed unilaterally shortly afterward that all French seminaries had to teach the Gallican Liberties as part of their theology course. Professors had to undertake to defend this view, and they had to submit their lectures for inspection by State officials. These officials also had access to the student's notes.

Restoration of the monarchy in 1814 brought no improvement. A generation had grown up in a secularist philosophy, which in freedom's name restricted freedom to statist ideologies and accorded the State the right to dictate the content of education. Accordingly, while Catholic educators were harassed in rebuilding a school system, they made little progress toward ending State control of the curriculum, even in seminaries.

The situation was further complicated by the fact that Gallicanism was within the Church as well as round about her. Even the superior at St. Vincent's, John Baptist Bouvier, a theologian of repute, had Gallican leanings. Some years later, when he had become Bishop of Le Mans, Rome seriously considered putting his theological writings on the Index but settled for expurgation. Basil's professor of theology, a Father Hamon, was thoroughly Gallican.

Despite these circumstances, Basil had no problem in choosing sides between France and the Holy See. He was a loyal Frenchman and always promoted his country's culture and civilization. But love for France did not blind him. It was balanced by love for Rome, a love derived from his parents and his earliest associations. This was one of the good things that resulted from the efforts during the Revolution to promote a schism. It forced the people to declare themselves. Though it was not recognized at the time, the Concordat symbolized the victory of the papacy and the death of Gallicanism.

This is not to say that Basil positively rejected the theses taught him at St. Vincent's. No evidence exists that he did other than accept without question the views presented by the professors. But when shortly he found himself in the more open academic atmosphere of St. Sulpice, he had little difficulty in recognizing and rejecting the errors he had been taught.

In the seminary, however, as throughout life, Basil was less concerned with the intellectual quest for knowledge than with the knowledge itself as a means to an end. He did not despise knowledge. On the contrary, he regarded it highly, and few in his or any generation did more to defend and diffuse it. A quick student, he studied with the energy and concentration with which he did everything. And he knew what he knew. "I taught theology," he told Cardinal Barnabo a little testily one day, when His Eminence questioned the correctness of a position he was maintaining. But his abiding sense of the urgency of a moral and spiritual restoration of society forced him to concentrate on the practical aspects of education. He was a man of action.

There is nothing to suggest that Basil ever doubted his call to the priesthood. The few letters and notes which survive from his seminary years reflect seriousness, sincerity, a touching affection for his family, and an untroubled sense of vocation. "Make things easy for our good mother," he wrote to his sister Victoire, adding a hope that they might be able to live with him "when I reach my goal." To his sister Cecile he wrote that he one day "felt a strong desire to go off into the desert," and that he hoped the same inspiration would often return, because it encouraged him in the practice of virtue. "Enjoy the pleasure of one of your sons called perhaps to fulfill the dread functions of the priesthood," he told his parents, "and perhaps also to give his life for the faith." The language is stiff, in the manner of the times, but the sentiment is sincere.

It seems that not enough attention is paid to the human elements in Father Moreau's personality. Recall the earlier references to the family spirit he breathed into his foundations. This was the key to all his personal relations. Thus, as a seminarian, we find him joining in and defending the laughter of the students, when with the maddening logic of the young they simultaneously discover some ludicrous element in a serious, possibly sacred occasion. He even succeeded in persuading a scandalized and long-faced newcomer that if uncontrollable laughter is a weakness, it must be recognized as "the sickness of the friends of God."

The personal magnetism which made him a leader as a boy and which would win disciples and helpers in extraordinary numbers throughout life excludes all possibility of an introverted or forbidding personality. Laughter would always flourish around him. Father Mollevaut was to write him in 1841, when he was novice master, approving what he had seen during a recent visit, and noting as a sure sign of a good spirit that the novices were like children and loved to laugh.

The recollections of a Brother who lived for many years with him bear out the same point. "Very Reverend Father Moreau was friendly with everybody," he wrote.

> On more than one occasion he was seen taking his place on a bench in the midst of the novices and coadjutor Brothers, to clean vegetables with them. It was on these occasions that Brother Marie Benoit, who was in charge of the vegetables, and who was from the same locality as Father Moreau, though a little bit older, took pleasure in recounting the little pranks which the Superior General had played on his mother and on others in his boyhood. Our good Father found this very interesting and laughed wholeheartedly. And we, the novices, how happy we were to hear the accounts of these little humorous incidents in the life of young Basil Moreau.

Another aspect of the friendliness of this austere man appears in a reflection written in 1858 by an architect reminiscing about a return visit to the high school where he had studied twelve years earlier under Father Moreau's direction. He mentions his emotion when he saw his former tutor. It was, he said, like seeing "an aged father after a long absence. . . . I ran towards him. . . . The sparkle in his eyes and his kindly smile did a world of good for my soul. I let myself be caught up in his arms."

Analyzing his affection for his former school, this observer singled out a feature which made it unique for the time. Instead of the military atmosphere then universal, with a gulf between professors and pupils as deep as that separating the officer caste from enlisted men in the army, Father Moreau had developed a family spirit. The teachers were concerned with every phase of their pupils' development, and they received in return the affection that is the reward of parents.

Another expression of the family spirit in the school was the "family council" composed of the parents of twelve pupils, which offered suggestions calculated to improve the school. It met regularly the day after the school year opened in October, in early January, at Pentecost, and on the second to last day of the school year, while extraordinary meetings could be summoned at other times. It discussed discipline, curricula, the physical and moral conditions, public opinion as it might affect the school, and relations between the students and the administration. This was undoubtedly a pioneer effort in parent-teacher associations and boards.

Father Moreau felt that nothing was good enough for others. He praised every effort of his companions and was quick to read the best interpretation into their actions. They could, and frequently did, take advantage of his readiness to impose intolerable burdens on himself in order to lighten theirs. "The good superior general," as his nephew once commented, "separated from his Council, could refuse nothing, provided his conscience did not place him under strict obligation."

A curious note is struck by his traveling companion in an account of the only trip he took to the United States. There are few situations which tend to bring out a person's qualities so rapidly as the confined society of a ship. The year was 1857, and they had a trying two weeks at sea, the vessel constantly pitching and dreadful night storms terrifying the passengers. Father Moreau welded together into a temporary community the fourteen religious from different congregations on board, organizing prayers and spiritual readings. He was calm and smiling at all times, and, as his companion reported, he charmed them all by his "marvelous lightheartedness."

Such characteristics would mark Basil Moreau throughout life, as they marked him in the seminary where he progressed rapidly through the prescribed courses. He received the subdiaconate in May 1820, the diaconate in April 1821, and the priesthood in August 1821. The dispensation because of age, for he lacked eighteen months of reaching the canonically required twenty-four years, was easily secured, both because of his intellectual and moral standing and because the diocese desperately needed priests.

He celebrated his first solemn Mass in his native village, assisted by the pastor who had taught him and encouraged his vocation. A neighboring pastor, another confessor of the Faith imprisoned during the Revolution, preached.

The whole family was present, father, mother, brothers, and sisters. No record of their emotions exists, but none is necessary. This was the moment for which their lives had been lived from the day Father Le Provost had persuaded them that it was possible and that it was God's will that their son and brother should become a priest. From that time, their previous Christian life had been intensified, so that they seemed to accompany him along the path of virtue and spirituality he had chosen. Whatever trials and crosses were to be his lot in life, none ever came from his dear ones. On the contrary, he was able to write Father Mollevaut the day after his mother's death four years later that "she died as she had lived, with sentiments of lively faith and perfect resignation to the orders of God."

Similarly, when the time came for his father to leave this world, the son was to be edified by like manifestations of spirituality. When they asked the old man, by now blind, how he was, he answered, "I must go to see God." A little later he added this prayer: "My God, may Your Gospel be preached in the entire world; may all my children sing Your praises, and may Your missionaries be everywhere welcomed." It was an anticipation of the part his priest-son would play in the years to follow.

CHAPTER THREE

Grace Builds on Nature

Basil Moreau possessed a major asset for his lifework. He had the ability of great men to reduce a situation to simple terms. He saw the world as a battlefield of good and evil, on which the age-old war had recently entered a phase of unusual fluidity. The forces of evil were in process of consolidating the major tactical gain they had just scored. The French Revolution had dethroned Christ and substituted Voltaire. The leaders, thinkers, educators, and politicians had bent the knee before the false gods. Failing decisive counteraction, the masses would follow.

Such was Basil Moreau's magnificently simple and accurate summation of the challenge presented him by life. His world was one of crisis and war. Unless the good moved quickly and decisively, France would be plunged into ignorance and atheism. It was necessary to recruit whatever soldiers one could round up and rush them into the line with whatever equipment and weapons they had handy. He knew it was not the best way, but what could he do? You must hold on, with bare hands if necessary, while a striking force is being assembled.

It was during his two years of study and prayer at St. Sulpice and the Solitude of Issy immediately after ordination that this vision of life took firm hold. But its outline was already forming while he was a seminarian, and his youthful enthusiasm urged him to direct and immediate action. Fortunately those around him had a clearer understanding of his potential. By holding him back, they helped in the development of situations which encouraged the creation of instruments to multiply and perpetuate his efforts.

The decision to send him to St. Sulpice was a great disappointment to Father Moreau, for his ambition was to train in the foreign mission seminary and preach the Gospel overseas. The bishop decided otherwise. He needed a professor for his major seminary, and Father Moreau was recommended as the most promising of his year.

It was a test of his spirit of obedience. He prized learning, which was to be a major aim of his foundations. He was particularly conscious of the need to train seminarians, since holy and learned priests were essential to the reform of society. But he felt called to help the masses by direct action. He was indeed destined to do this, and to an extent greater than he could have dreamed. But he first had to learn a mystery of life, that the grain of wheat must fall into the earth and be consumed before it can produce a hundredfold.

An intimate, self-evaluating letter to Father Louis Jean Fillion, his friend and confessor at the seminary, expresses something of his disappointment. If only the bishop had let him hide himself in a country parish, he wrote, then hastened to assure his spiritual guide that he would do whatever he was told.

Such obedience would characterize his life. It becomes more striking when contrasted with the experience he would frequently have from others equally pledged to obey, even from religious subject to the vow of obedience. His was the age of revolt. His lifetime saw the universal acceptance of what were proclaimed as the principles but were often the shibboleths of liberty and equality. It took a remarkable man to accept these principles, as he did, and still reconcile them with the apparently conflicting and widely despised principle of obedience.

Whatever Father Moreau may have thought at the time, the favor the bishop did him in sending him to St. Sulpice soon became evident. The Sulpicians were the ones who in France carried out a major wish of the Council of Trent, by giving a stable and definitive form to the program of training priests. The ecclesiastical formation they offered was methodical, detailed, exhaustive, and inspired by an incomparable sense of the grandeur and sacredness of the priesthood.

The Sulpician spirit had survived the Revolution. Father Moreau found at St. Sulpice the traditional atmosphere of infinite politeness, simplicity, a self-control for which any outburst was in bad taste, a continual support of the supernatural by the natural virtues, an ability to adjust to all surroundings, and a breadth of interest.

Even more important, he found these qualities incarnated in a man to whom he took to instinctively and who in turn understood the tremendous possibilities for spiritual development hidden behind the simple exterior of a peasant boy just starting on the great adventure of life as a priest. Father Mollevaut crossed Father Moreau's path at a critical moment, and his influence was more profound than that of any other in the shaping of Father Moreau's entire career.

Here was a man to fire the imagination of any youth, this superior at the Solitude of Issy. He was tall, broad-shouldered, deep-chested, with tireless feet and strong arms, and he loved fresh air and liked to work in the garden with a shovel and rake. His blue eyes were filled with calm and piety, to quote an observer, and over his whole face a restful, holy, and heavenly expression. He was a marvelous combination of politeness, affability, and meekness.

And what a legend to fit this figure! The son of a nobleman who was a deputy to the Convention of 1790, Gabriel Mollevaut had listened with his father to the orators of the Revolution in the Assembly and the clubs, and at the family table. After some hesitation, Mollevaut senior supported the King and fled to escape the guillotine.

The son escaped with the father and joined the cavalry under an assumed name. After an interval, he resumed his higher studies, then attached himself to an Italian supporter of Napoleon who soon became head of the Transalpine Republic and sent him as his ambassador to Paris.

It was a position to which the twenty-five year-old Gabriel was eminently suited. He had been a brilliant student, equally at home in the humanities and mathematics. Already he was acquiring the fame of being one of the most learned of living Greek scholars. He spoke five modern languages, including Russian. He had exquisite tastes. His views were valued in the world of arts and letters.

From diplomacy he passed to teaching, acquiring new fame as professor of Greek, Latin, and Italian at the College of Metz. In the classroom he remained standing and always wore evening dress: black cutaway, an elaborate lace ruffle on his shirt-front, buckled shoes, white silk stockings. He was an intellectual aristocrat.

After nearly ten years of this success, a more radical change began to occur. Mollevaut had grown up in a religious atmosphere and had even thought of becoming a priest, but as a student he had accepted the godless influences to which he was exposed. He never lost his faith or led a dissolute life, but he ceased completely to practice his religion.

Now grace began to recover the upper hand. He went to Mass every morning. His dress became simple. Soon he grew active in good works. When an outbreak of typhus occurred, he nursed the sick and prayed with the dying.

It was but a short step from here to a monastery. His spiritual director recommended the Sulpicians, who welcomed him without apparently knowing how distinguished their forty-one year-old novice was. He began to lead an austere and humble life, with no reference to his influential acquaintances, his erudition, or his talents. The talents, however, could not remain hidden. Ordained in 1816, he was appointed superior of the Solitude of Issy three years later and held the position for eighteen years.

Soon his prestige brought priests from all over France who, like Father Moreau, were picked by their bishops to be professors and ultimately superiors of seminaries. At Issy they got not only higher learning but the Sulpician spirituality in which Father Mollevaut had steeped himself in a very short time.

There was nothing harsh about the man. His aristocratic and diplomatic manner never left him, but he did insist strongly on external training and strict observance of rules. He stressed silence as the basic guarantee of the interior life, early rising, evening examination of conscience, and the monthly retreat.

Father Mollevaut's experience made him emphasize the amount of time needed to create a thoroughly spiritual outlook. "In practically all those who finish in even the best of seminaries," he said, "the interior man is hardly more than roughly sketched." Hence, he urged the young priests who passed through Issy to continue after they left in the practice of the exercises of piety to which he had initiated them.

He always found time to stay in touch with those who sought to develop the interior life. He followed them in their ministry, encouraging them, correcting them, answering their questions, clarifying their doubts, and rekindling their zeal. In 1837, when he was sixty-four, he was relieved of his post at Issy at his own request, because his health no longer allowed him to give it the attention he felt it needed. However, retirement did not end activity. He traveled through France, visiting seminaries and meeting the men he had trained, a work he continued until his mind began to give way twelve years later. He was eighty when he died in 1854.

The perspective on life and providence of such a man, who was forty-two when he was ordained and forty-five when he began his life's work, was of particular value to an impetuous youth like Basil Moreau, driven by an almost irresistible sense of urgency into a multiplicity of activities that might easily have frittered away his talents. He never changed Basil's temperament, nor indeed did he want to. His purpose was only to slow him down, to give him time to acquire a maturity of outlook and a supernaturalness of judgment.

The history of the development of Holy Cross would show how right Father Mollevaut was. Among Father Moreau's colleagues, there would be not a few who could be compared with him for their zeal and their dedication, but none received a spiritual formation as deep or so extended as his. They were plunged into the active ministry right away, and many of them were given positions of authority before they had learned how to obey. Their mistakes caused great harm to the Congregation. If the founder had not achieved so complete a control over his natural reactions, they might easily have destroyed it.

St. Sulpice was also Father Moreau's first exposure to a stimulating intellectual atmosphere. In contrast to his earlier experience of passive assimilation of predigested answers, he was now asking and being asked questions. The opponents were no longer bowling pins set up in order to be knocked down but intellectual swordsmen who yielded only to superior skill and resource.

Father Moreau and his contemporaries were less interested in theory than in action. They belonged to a generation which thought it had all the answers. People had taken sides, and it seemed more important to help those on your side to defend themselves than to engage in futile debate on mutually exclusive principles.

At St. Sulpice, Father Moreau showed little interest in the issues separating the Church from the militantly anti-Catholic liberals who dominated secular society. The students of theology were allowed to attend lectures at the Sorbonne, but after listening to a couple of them, he had had enough. He agreed that some ought to engage in this debate, but for himself it was a "pure waste of time."

What did interest him was the internal strengthening of the Church, and what captured his imagination was the Gallican controversy, which he correctly identified as a major threat to the purity of the faith. French theologians had long since retreated from the extreme positions established a century and a half earlier, but even a leading thinker like the superior at St. Vincent's could defend a modified version that would give the bishops almost complete independence of the Holy See in the sphere of Church organization and administration.

Strong support for such an attitude existed at St. Sulpice too, but Father Moreau rallied quickly to the other side, thanks—at least in part—to a bold and original thinker under whose influence he had just come. "I have never taken so many notes," he wrote from St. Sulpice in March 1822, in the course of a letter, which dealt at length with the theories of Lamennais.

It was an extraordinary experience for Father Moreau not only to move from the unquestioning attitude of acceptance which had characterized the seminary classroom to the critical atmosphere of St. Sulpice but to find that the very positions previously taken for granted were all challenged by the man held here in highest esteem. For the *Essay on Indifference*, which had rocketed Lamennais into prominence with the publication of the two first volumes in 1817 and 1820, grappled precisely with the deep roots of rationalism, challenging Descartes, rejecting Gallicanism, and championing papal infallibility and the primacy of the Church's spiritual power.

Father Moreau followed the discussion with extreme interest. The stress on the rights of the Holy See fit perfectly with his own emotional position and helped to arouse his enthusiasm for the ideas set forth by this romantic philosopher with a brilliant style and exposition. Nevertheless, he was not entirely convinced. Time and again, he sought from Father Mollevaut an approval for his own urge to identify himself publicly as a supporter of Lamennais. But his prudent spiritual director held him back, and he certainly did not follow Lamennais in his intellectual development from conservative traditionalism to revolutionary democracy. He grieved indeed when Lamennais was condemned by the Holy See and failed to submit, but the ruling created no personal problem for him. His one regret was that he had even taken sides in the controversy at an earlier date, and for this he apologized to his colleagues at St. Vincent's Seminary at the earliest opportunity.

The intellectual encounter with Lamennais was, of course, not as important in Father Moreau's evolution as his meeting with Father Mollevaut and his choice of him as spiritual director. Nevertheless, it complemented that decisive event, placing him openly on the side of Rome. If this position was to make enemies and cause him great sufferings through the years, it was also to save him in moments of crisis. For only intense devotion to the Holy See and unquestioning acceptance of its authority could maintain the blind obedience which was more than once required. Only a rejection of the harsh Jansenistic approach to the confessional and to the care of souls could make fruitful the life of the missionary and director of religious communities.

Father Moreau was an enthusiastic and successful student. He had a clear, retentive mind and an ability to appreciate a viewpoint he did not share. He was also an incredibly hard worker. Within two short years he became sufficiently proficient in Hebrew to translate prayers, which he later incorporated in a community prayerbook. Hebrew was for him a tool to a more complete mastery of Sacred Scripture, a subject he later taught. His familiarity with Scripture, reflected in letters, sermons, and writings, was truly phenomenal. It constituted a basic element in his own spiritual life and in his apostolic influence.

At St. Sulpice and during the following years devoted to teaching philosophy, theology, and Scripture, Father Moreau always felt that his true vocation lay elsewhere. Father Mollevaut simultaneously encouraged this aspiration to work in a broader field and discouraged immediate or abrupt change. Obedience, he insisted, had determined his state, and if it was God's will, obedience would alter it.

How much he took this advice to heart is revealed by correspondence with his friend and former confessor, Father Fillion, who had been named superior of the seminary at Tessé. Knowing that Father Fillion was well aware of his personal preferences, and that he was also in a position to influence the bishop in deciding what assignment to give Father Moreau at the end of his course at St. Sulpice, he wrote to urge Father Fillion on no account to intervene on his behalf. I want to do whatever the superiors decide, he insisted, without having their judgment influenced by the injection of my own wishes.

While making headway in virtue, Father Moreau was acquiring a more intimate and personal understanding of the society which he felt called to reform. Gradually the major elements took clear shape in his mind and along with them the techniques by which the bad could be combated and the good strengthened.

Liberalism characterized public life in nineteenth-century France, but a liberalism very different from what the word today connotes. It was militantly anti-Catholic and often based its political tenets on a philosophy incompatible not only with Catholicism but with any supernatural view of life. The so-called modern conscience offered not merely an alternative to the traditional viewpoint but a direct challenge. Its proclaimed purpose was to eliminate what it called the relics of the Dark Ages.

This analysis of the dogmatic stand of the antidogmatists is necessary for a perspective on Father Moreau and on the nineteenth-century Catholic position. Far from adopting any position of practical neutrality between conflicting theories, or of joining opponents in defending the freedom of each to hold what was believed to be subjectively true, Father Moreau's enemies wanted nothing less than a denial of the objective truth that the Church affirmed.

Seen in this light, the Church was undergoing an active persecution. It was of a kind new to Father Moreau and his contemporaries, but it was not new to the Church, since it was in essence a revival of that conducted by Julian the Apostate—a historic figure who was in fact idolized by the anticlericals.

The practical program of these sectarians, who dominated France for most of the nineteenth and into the twentieth centuries, was to create political and cultural conditions which would bring about the disappearance from society of what they called "a residue of intolerance." Catholicism, they taught, was not adaptable to progress. It should be denied all participation in education and culture. In effect, they sought an Inquisition in reverse, excluding the Catholic from social action as representing a prescientific mentality.

The Jesuits were the focal point of attack, both because they led in defending the Church's right and ability to survive in the modern world, and because they did most to adjust the Church attitudes and structures to new conditions. The anticlericals feared less a reactionary Church operating and thinking in terms of a different age than an up-to-date Church purged of the defects which had weakened her position. Regardless of their professed principles, they had tactically to be Gallicans, for the Roman party inside the Church promised new strength and vitality.

In every move to renew some element of religious life they saw the hidden hand of the Jesuits, and they counterattacked with a scurrility and disregard for fact which showed they had taken to heart Voltaire's counsel to "lie, friends, lie, not timidly, but outrageously, like the devil."

Time and again, Father Moreau suffered smear tactics, denounced as a crypto-Jesuit and accused of wanting to re-establish under various disguises the hated Society of Jesus. His calumniators were perhaps closer to the truth than they knew, for he was deeply influenced by Ignatian spirituality, drew heavily on the rule of the Society for the constitutions of his foundations, and promoted the Jesuit concept of obedience by instructing each of his subjects to read, on the monthly retreat day, St. Ignatius's letter on obedience.

CHAPTER FOUR

Teacher, Organizer, Leader

F ather Moreau knew, when he was sent to St. Sulpice, that he was being prepared for a career as a seminary professor. The assignment terrified him. Not only was he disappointed at the unwillingness of his bishop to send him to the foreign missions, he was worried that he lacked the aptitudes and the virtues needed to train seminarians.

When the time came to begin the task, however, he threw himself into it with his entire energy. He was greatly helped by Father Mollevaut, to whom he submitted all his problems, and from whom he received a wealth of wise guidance in both intellectual and moral matters. The result was that his work was crowned with notable success as a professor, as an administrator, and as a spiritual guide to the seminarians.

His first assignment was as professor of philosophy at the minor seminary of Tessé, in 1823, where he had the great satisfaction of working under his friend, Father Fillion. Two years later he was advanced to the chair of dogmatic theology in the major seminary of St. Vincent's, under the same Father Bouvier who had been his superior when he was a student there.

The solidity of the foundations laid at St. Sulpice soon became evident. He was a dedicated and successful teacher and administrator, and the steady increase in his responsibilities marked him for a brilliant professional career. Even his vacations were utilized to increase his intellectual contacts and promote his spiritual advancement. In 1826, for example, he made a long trip through Savoy, spending seventeen days at the Grande Chartreuse, during which he made his annual retreat. On this trip, too, he made the acquaintance of a Father Favre, a pastoral theologian of some prominence. Father Favre was then writing a book on the sacrament of penance, in which he urged confessors to adopt the antirigorist views of St. Alphonsus Liguori. Father Moreau's subsequent correspondence with Father Mollevaut shows that they both read this book and regarded it highly.

La Trappe was another favorite place for Father Moreau to make his retreat. He was there in 1824 and again in 1829, while he returned to the Solitude of Issy for his 1831 retreat. Always, in addition to the spiritual renewal, he took advantage of these trips to develop friendships with priests who shared his intellectual and social interests.

Nevertheless, during the thirteen years he spent in teaching, he never felt he was achieving everything of which he was capable in God's service. He reconciled himself to the fact that obedience had determined that this was what he had to do here and now. But he saw a future in which wider perspectives might open for him, and he worked constantly to prepare himself and the circumstances for that day.

In addition to dedication and energy, he had an ability to organize men and material resources and direct them to a defined purpose. And he knew that a few people, properly trained and led, can alter the course of human affairs, for better no less than for worse. What was needed was a simple strategy and a unity of direction to put that strategy into effect.

What was his strategy? As he saw it, the thing that would do most for religion was a wider diffusion of knowledge. His personal devotion to the Holy Trinity made his thinking and action run in triads, and he projected religious knowledge on three levels: the highest possible professional studies for priests and teachers, a network of religiously oriented schools for primary and secondary pupils, and Christian teaching to adults by priests who would go from parish to parish preaching missions.

Father Moreau was a practical man. When he set himself these aims, he was thinking both of what should be done and what was concretely possible. And he saw that his aims could be achieved only by creating organizations which by uniting efforts and minds could multiply his individual efforts a hundred and a thousandfold.

The apostle in Father Moreau wanted to plunge directly into the job, but the business executive knew that it required this multiplication of energies. Organization became accordingly the keynote of his apostolate. All through life, he would found, inspire, mold organizations.

As already noted, he started with no preconceived idea that he was called to be a founder. Rather, he found himself time and again in circumstances that needed an organization. If one was available, he used or adapted it. If not, he created it. Indeed, he thought seriously for a time of joining an existing religious body and working through it. About eight years after his ordination and six after he had left St. Sulpice, he wrote his spiritual director that he felt strongly urged to become a Sulpician.

Father Mollevaut's first reaction was favorable. Nevertheless, he counseled patience and warned against a change motivated by dissatisfaction with the conditions in which he had to work. Father Fillion confirmed this viewpoint, and he continued to teach.

Other developments, however, were foreshadowing the end of his professorial career. One such occurred in 1830. The controversy on Gallicanism had entered an acute stage, and it was being fought within St. Vincent's seminary as all over France. The state authorities insisted that Napoleon's decree obliging all seminaries to accept and teach the Gallican Declaration of 1682 remained in full force. Father Felicité de Lamennais got into trouble with the police for his book published in 1825–26 on the relations of religion with the civil political order. The work was seized, and he was fined.

As professor of dogmatic theology, Father Moreau could not avoid involvement. Convinced that the Gallican position was theologically unsound, he backed Lamennais. Such a stand was, nevertheless, embarrassing. The Bishop of Le Mans belonged to the old school, and so did the seminary superior, Father Bouvier, a scholar with national prestige.

Rumors circulated that the Government would require seminary professors to sign statements accepting the Declaration, a step Father Moreau was not prepared to take. The Minister of Ecclesiastical Affairs, a bishop, added to the confusion by getting several fellow bishops to publish a manifesto that, while they acknowledged "the primacy of St. Peter and the Roman pontiffs, his successors," they condemned "the censures hurled without reason and without authority" against "certain principles accepted in the Church of France."

That Father Moreau was agitated is clear from his letters. Father Mollevaut, however, insisted on calm, urging him not to anticipate a dilemma that might never arise, and which in fact never did. While the civil authorities hesitated, the July Revolution of 1830 put an end to Charles X's dream of a restoration of absolutism.

By this time an important change had occurred in Father Moreau's situation. In March he had been informed that he was to teach scripture instead of dogmatic theology. This was welcome news. He loved the subject and was well equipped to teach it. But the motive hurt him. Everyone knew that the seminary superior, Father Bouvier, was taking this way to silence his criticism of the Gallican viewpoint. Father Moreau respected Father Bouvier, but he could never compromise when he believed a principle was involved, no matter what the consequences. His inability to regain the confidence of Father Bouvier was to hurt increasingly, for he was named Bishop of Le Mans in 1833 and for twenty-one years exercised a veto over Father Moreau's actions.

Father Moreau was distressed, but he didn't sulk. Instead, he plunged into other activities. So it will always be—as one door closes, he opens another.

The door he now opened was in fact wider than he or any of the others involved could have foreseen at the time. By answering an appeal from one of his fellow priests to lend a hand to a small community of teaching Brothers he was starting on a road at the end of which would one day rise the Congregation of Holy Cross.

To understand how this came about, it is necessary to know something of the career of this fellow priest.

The life of Jacques Dujarié is the history in miniature of the Church in France during and immediately after the Revolution. Born in 1767, he spent his early years as a student and seminarian far removed from the turmoil and violence rocking the capital and shaking the social system.

He was twenty-four and a deacon when events caught up with him and forced him to decide. The seminary was closed and the students dispersed when the directors refused to take the schismatic oath. Young Dujarié did not hesitate. He joined the underground clergy who managed everywhere to maintain contacts with the faithful and provide the essentials of religion.

After moving from place to place for four years, he attached himself to the pastor of a village named Ruillé, was secretly ordained, and exercised his underground ministry until the signing of the Concordat of 1801. Two years later he became pastor of Ruillé, and there he spent the rest of his active life.

Father Dujarié had already won the good will of his parishioners. A meeting of the village council called to fix his salary singled out three qualities: that he used his own money to buy what was needed for religious services, that he taught the children without charge, and that he helped the poor to the extent of his small resources.

The people had sized up the new pastor well. He had a deep sense of his duty to his parishioners. One of his first undertakings was a charity center at Ruillé, which he got a small community of nuns to supervise. The Sisters cared for the sick and taught the children. The condition of the young was deplorable, especially in outlying parts of the parish, where many lived in a state of semisavagery. Father Dujarié started a second school in a village some miles from Ruillé, where he put girls in charge who gradually formed a religious community under the title of Sisters of Providence.

These developments were taking place under the improved climate that followed the downfall of Napoleon and the restoration of the Bourbons in the person of Louis XVIII. The new king sought to steer a middle course. He guaranteed the status, titles, and privileges of the upper middle class, which had become the dominant sociopolitical force under Napoleon, by adopting a Constitution that was technically democratic but actually reserved power to the wealthy. But he naturally tried within this framework to restore some of the benefits stripped by the Revolution from the old upper classes and the Church.

Specifically as regards the Church, he did not attempt to abrogate the restrictive laws or amend the Concordat, but he sought to develop more favorable administrative interpretations. Napoleon had created a rigid monopoly of secondary and higher education by reorganizing the university as a centrally controlled institution and making all colleges, lyceums, and faculties dependent on it. Louis XVIII did not touch the monopoly, but he introduced ecclesiastics into teaching and administrative posts to balance the anticlericals who had previously had things all to themselves.

Religious orders and congregations still had no legal status and could not own property or openly direct teaching establishments, but now they were permitted to function through administrative connivance. Working solutions were found to the practical problems. Property was put in the names of trusted individuals, or members of a community formed a civil society (a kind of business partnership) to hold property. Such devices allowed charitable and educational organizations to function, though they did not give complete protection. For example, the heirs could upset a legacy in favor of a civil society if they proved it was a device to evade the law forbidding gifts to religious organizations. Father Moreau would later be victimized by this provision, as well as by liability for debts on community property of which he was legally the owner.

Despite the obstacles, the Sisters of Providence had grown to fifty by 1826, and they were recognized by the Government as a charitable organization dedicated to teaching. This limited approval did not create full civil personality. Legacies or donations for their benefit could not be given directly to them. They had to be made to the Royal University of France, which administered them in conformity with the intentions of the donors. Nevertheless, it greatly strengthened the situation of the group.

A few years earlier, Father Dujarié had become involved in a still more ambitious project. In 1818, the clergy of the diocese of Le Mans assembled for a retreat for the first time since the Revolution. All had the same basic problem, to rebuild the ruins, and all agreed that an element demanding immediate action was the religious ignorance into which their flocks had fallen.

The Brothers of the Christian Schools, founded by St. John Baptist de la Salle (popularly known in the United States as the Christian Brothers), had been suppressed at the Revolution. In 1808, Napoleon had authorized them to reopen their houses, though under a regulatory system which in effect made the chief government inspector of schools their superior. Their expansion, however, was slow, because they properly insisted on adequate training of candidates. Their rule, in addition, prescribed that they could make no charge for education and that not fewer than three brothers should form a house. Many pastors did not have the financial resources to operate a school on these terms. The consequence was that by 1815 the restored Christian Brothers had not more than forty schools in all of France.

Many dioceses in the west of France began immediately after the Restoration to establish their own associations of teaching brothers, modeled in general after the Christian Brothers, and it was decided at the time of the 1818 clergy retreat that Le Mans should do the same.

The choice fell on Father Dujarié, for everyone was talking about the success of his charity center and the growth of the Sisters of Providence. The new superior of the seminary, Father Bouvier, was particularly insistent, and his backing ensured the support of all the priests. Father Dujarié agreed.

Two years later, in the summer of 1820, the first brothers were installed in Father Dujarié's rectory. Their rules were based on those of the Brothers of Brittany, recently established by Father Jean Marie de Lamennais. Brother André Mottais, a promising recruit, went for training to the novitiate of the Christian Brothers at Paris and brought back their methods and books. The spirituality and dedication of Brother André were to serve the group well.

Pastors who wanted schools sent candidates from all over the diocese. By 1823, when the State recognized them as a "charitable association for the advancement of elementary education," there were thirty brothers and ten schools. The backing of the entire diocese gave the work a tremendous impetus, raising the number of subjects to more than a hundred in a few years.

But Father Dujarié was under no illusion. He knew that behind the façade there was a great emptiness. Here was a situation quite different from that of the Sisters of Providence. When he started the Sisters in 1806, he was only thirty-nine. He was strong and healthy, able to provide for both material and spiritual needs of the community. The first superior had proved to be a trouble-maker, but he was able to stop her quickly. Then he had the good fortune to recruit two girls who combined administrative talent and spiritual dedication. Under their guidance, the congregation had gotten on its own feet. Its future was assured.

When the Brothers started in 1820, on the other hand, Father Dujarié was already fifty-three and a sick man. Besides, the external pressures made him move too fast. Candidates arrived with high enthusiasm and almost no preparation. Some were practically illiterate. During a brief novitiate before going off to take charge of a school, they had to learn the rudiments of reading, writing, and arithmetic, as well as some basic concepts of the devout life. Brother André was an excellent novice master, but there was a limit to what he could do.

The very nature of their vocation created great stresses for the Brothers. Unlike the Sisters of Providence grouped together in their convent, many of them lived alone or with a single companion in a village school. If they were good teachers, they quickly became important in the community. It was easy for them to neglect their devotions and to develop ambitions at variance with their work.

Father Dujarié believed he knew what would supply the needed internal strength and cohesion. He made two separate efforts to organize a society of diocesan priests as an intellectual and moral nucleus, an idea which was being tried by other superiors of newly formed groups of teaching brothers with whom he was in contact—for example, Father Deshayes and Father de Lamennais. By doing so, they sought to achieve a double benefit, to provide continuity of spiritual direction and to create a committee or society that could legally hold the community's property and that would be composed of individuals whose sacred calling guaranteed their lifelong commitment.

Father Dujarié's idea was right. It would later be taken up by Father Moreau and help determine the organizational structure of the Congregation of Holy Cross. But Father Dujarié's age and infirmity prevented him from carrying it out, and he himself knew he was beaten when, in 1830, the repercussions of the July Revolution caused the entire structure to totter. An upsurge of anticlericalism made some fear the approach of a new persecution. More than fifty Brothers abandoned their posts, and out of the sixty-eight who were still teaching at the end of the year, only eight had renewed the annual vow of obedience which was the sole bond holding the group together.

But Father Dujarié had great faith. Despite sickness, he was still the same determined man who had never abandoned his post during the Terror. At that time, the village council had testified to his selflessness, and now once more in his old age he exhibited precisely the same characteristic. Recognizing that he was no longer fit for the task, he looked for somebody to whom it might be handed over.

The man he picked was Father Moreau, and events were to confirm his good judgment. They had known each other since 1823, when the Bishop had sent Father Moreau to conduct the Brothers' retreat at Ruillé. Perhaps then or subsequently, they had exchanged views on forming a society of diocesan priests, a project that was already in Father Moreau's mind at St. Sulpice.

When they met in 1831 on Father Dujarié's initiative to discuss the situation, the two men found themselves in perfect agreement, both on short-range action to avert collapse, and on long-range changes to create a structure capable of sanctifying its members and serving the Church not only in Le Mans but throughout France and around the world. The measure of Father Dujarié's understanding and holiness is his willingness to hand over his work ungrudgingly to his successor. Like John the Baptist, he realized that his task was to prepare the way. Like John, he proclaimed at the predestined moment that his part was accomplished and that the time had arrived to make way for one who would perfect the work.

Moving into action with the suavity of an efficiency expert, Father Moreau quickly revealed the ability to achieve a team response which would characterize his administration in later years. The immediate problem was to stop the panic and hold together the nucleus of the group. This he did by drawing up a pledge of fidelity, the signers of which undertaking to reassemble when possible if forced to disband. Fifteen signed, enough to restore confidence. There was no further talk of dissolution.

Father Moreau turned next to internal reform. Agreeing with Father Dujarié that the loose organization and inadequate spiritual training constituted a dangerous weakness, he decided that only the basic structure of the religious life, with its traditional characteristics, could cure these failings. He saw, however, that not all the Brothers were prepared to take the religious vows of poverty, chastity, and obedience. But a few were ready, and he could start with them.

It is significant to find at this early stage in Father Moreau's career a clear understanding of the need for personal sanctification as a basis for an external apostolate and a reasoned conviction that the religious state was the way to achieve that sanctification. Father Dujarié, Father de Lamennais, and other founders of groups of brothers and sisters were thinking mainly of recruiting personnel to respond to urgent needs. Father de Lamennais, for example, distributed his first associates right away in parish schools. Father Dujarié had not gone much further. He established a novitiate, but his motivation in doing so was at least as much to give future teachers a grounding in elementary education as to promote their spiritual formation. The novitiate was certainly not regarded by him as the gateway to the religious state. As late as 1834, he could write the bishop that after two years of formation the brothers had the practice of making an annual vow of obedience but that not all of them by any means took even this vow.

Father Moreau's greater stress on the primacy of personal sanctification and the importance of the religious state reflects his Sulpician training. It was a subject to which Father Mollevaut frequently returned in his letters, as in the following passage which synthesizes his thought:

> For an association, it is particularly the heart which must be formed, exercized and strengthened by virtue, and to accomplish all that, as experience proves, a single year of solitude is not very much. A man can do whatever he wants, but no one can produce a saint on the spur of the moment; and without sanctity, even with the best of dispositions, we cannot count on any success.

Father Moreau, accordingly, drafted a letter in which for the first time the brothers asked the bishop to authorize them to take the vows of religion. He followed this up, in 1832, with a detailed program of reform, under which he would become their spiritual director. His several letters to the bishop on this subject reveal a grasp of the situation, an understanding of the human elements involved, a feeling for what was practically possible, and a sensitivity toward recognizing and safeguarding Father Dujarié's rights, giving him full credit for what he had achieved, and maintaining his authority and dignity. Father Moreau was no brash young man moving in to clean up a mess. On the contrary, he showed an exquisite appreciation of the sensibilities of the older priest who had requested help.

Bishop Carron died in August 1833, without reaching a decision. Bishop Bouvier, his successor, had already begun to establish the ambivalent relationship with Father Moreau which would continue to the end. But as far as Father Dujarié was concerned, the new Bishop was entirely for him. He had been a sponsor of the institute of teaching Brothers, and the results they had achieved had confirmed his initial attitude. He therefore gladly approved the plan to restore them.

The steps Father Moreau had taken were already producing results. Brother André was promoting the reform with his colleagues, and his words carried more weight because of his training with the Christian Brothers. With the approval of Fathers Moreau and Dujarié, he wrote asking Bishop Bouvier to investigate in person and correct abuses. Also with Father Duja-rié's approval, he recommended Father Moreau as the man to affect the reforms.

For his part, Father Moreau was willing, provided he got full freedom, and provided also that the administrative center and novitiate were transferred to Le Mans. As seminary professor and assistant superior, he could not live elsewhere. The Brothers, he said, could have a house at Le Mans, which had been donated to him to be used at his discretion for a pious purpose.

All concerned were delighted. The Bishop presented the plan to the Brothers assembled for their annual retreat, and on August 31, 1835, Father Dujarié resigned so that the Bishop might appoint Father Moreau superior. The novitiate moved to Le Mans. Later, Father Dujarié resigned as pastor of Ruillé and spent his last days in this small community that was to become the mother house of a great religious congregation.

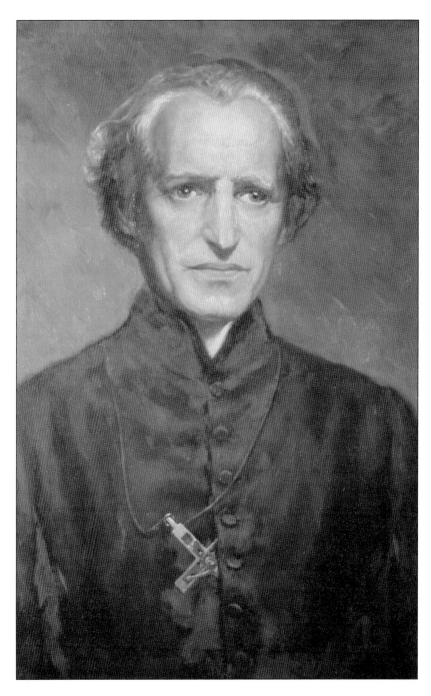

Father Basil Moreau

The main altar in the church where Basil Moreau was baptized at Lagné-en-balin, the town where he was born in 1799.

The second-level room where Moreau slept as a boy, located above the wine cellar owned by his father, a wine merchant.

Former seminary at Chateau-Gontier, where Moreau attended high
school.

Chapel of the Visitation church in Le Mans, where Moreau was ordained in 1821.

The church at Yvres l'eveque near Le Mans where Father Moreau performed his final apostolic mission and celebrated his final Mass.

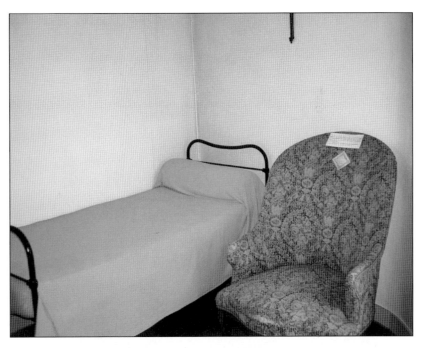

The bed in which Basil Moreau died in 1873 near the College de Notre Dame in Le Mans. Up until days before his death, Moreau had been sleeping for the previous twenty-five years in the chair shown here.

Basil Moreau's tomb in the crypt under the main altar at Notre Dame de Sainte-Croix in Le Mans.

CHAPTER FIVE

At Loggerheads with a Saint

The pattern of Father Moreau's later life was beginning to reveal itself. While dedicating what by any normal standard would be called his full-time energies to the work assigned to him by obedience, and doing that work superbly, he was finding ways to undertake important additional activities.

The reorganization of the Brothers of St. Joseph and the development of fund-raising techniques to support them was only one of these. It was time-consuming, and so was his work at the seminary, which involved a full teaching schedule, as well as the administrative and training functions of assistant superior. With all of that, he was becoming involved in two still further undertakings.

One was the creation of a group of diocesan missionaries. This was a project to which he had given considerable thought from his first days as a priest, and he was constantly casting about for ways to bring it to realization. At one point he thought of using his organization of priests to promote the generalate of the Good Shepherd, which Mother Pelletier was trying to establish. Later, he would bring them into a corporate association with the Brothers of St. Joseph in the Congregation of Holy Cross.

The other was the establishment of a convent of Good Shepherd sisters at Le Mans to take charge of an orphanage and a home for penitents. Both the civil and religious authorities of the city were interested in this venture. The long years of unrest and almost universal lack of religious training had created a situation in which homeless girls easily drifted into loose habits, and one of the first efforts of the Catholic revival in the social field was to create shelters for them.

For several years, two ladies of Le Mans had been trying to persuade the Good Shepherd Convent at Tours to make a foundation in their city. The initial response was favorable, but the Tours community decided instead to open a house at Angers, and there were not enough Sisters available to undertake two foundations simultaneously.

The Le Mans ladies, though disappointed, did not abandon their idea. The Angers house developed rapidly under the guidance of a young, energetic, and holy superior, Mother Euphrasia Pelletier. She was destined to become famous as the foundress of an important congregation and to achieve still wider fame when the church placed its formal seal on her holiness through canonization. In 1832, the Le Mans ladies approached Father Moreau to interest him in their project and persuade him to ask Mother Euphrasia if her convent would help them.

The suggestion appealed to him, and he immediately began to develop a concrete plan, which included looking for a house in which to install them, arranging for its remodeling when found, and raising enough money to pay a year's rent. Things had progressed far enough by the following February for Mother Euphrasia to meet Bishop Carron at Le Mans and reach an agreement fixing the opening date for the first week of May. Actually, the plans were pressed so ardently by all concerned that the opening took place ahead of schedule, with the arrival of four sisters in April.

As Father Moreau had arranged everything, it was natural that the Bishop should choose him as ecclesiastical superior of the foundation. This pleased everyone except himself. The Bishop had to assure Mother Euphrasia that Father Moreau would continue to be responsible for the community. "He is a child of obedience," he told her. "He will do whatever I order him to do, and I have already told him that I will not allow him to escape the burden which, out of modesty, he seemed unwilling to assume."

Mother Euphrasia's satisfaction was expressed in turn in a letter to the young sister she had placed in charge of the Le Mans community. "We cannot be grateful enough to our Lord," she wrote her. "And as for Father Moreau! The more I see of the marvels he has accomplished, the more I feel he is a saint, chosen from on high to be our founder and father. We must give him all our confidence."

No sooner had the group been installed than Father Moreau set to work to create a regular source of income both for the community itself and for the orphanage it had begun to establish. It is noteworthy that he turned not to the wealthy but to the poor, reading aright the signs of the times. The Church could not continue to look primarily to the rich to supply her needs. One of the positive results of upheaval and revolution was the emergence of the middle class as the dominant element in society. Ways would have to be found to enlist its support.

The plan he adopted was a mass organization to be called the Association of the Good Shepherd, an approach which may very well have been suggested to him by the Association for the Propagation of the Faith, which had been organized in France in 1822–23. At any rate, his Association of the Good Shepherd had a marked resemblance to it both in purpose and structure. It sought, as a matter of principle, to give the members a sense of participation in the work of the orphanage. They undertook specific spiritual obligations, a daily prayer, and an annual retreat, and they gave five sous monthly. The amount did not burden even the poor, but it sufficed by multiplication. Twenty associates provided funds to admit a penitent to the refuge. Thirty took care of an orphan.

Only six years after diocesan approval, the Association was collecting 42,405 francs, which at 60 sous annually per member indicates the active participation of more than 70,000 contributors. The equivalent in dollars at the exchange rates then prevailing would be slightly over 8,000. To establish a real value is more difficult, but some idea can be gained from the fact that it was possible to buy a permanent home for the convent, within a year of its establishment, for 60,000 francs. The property was on the site of an ancient abbey close to the city, and it consisted of five acres with three buildings.

Three of the four sisters who made the foundation were very young. Actually, although neither the Bishop of Le Mans nor Father Moreau knew this, these three, one of whom was named superior, had just made their first profession, and they had not even completed the regular novitiate, having been professed ahead of time with a dispensation from the Bishop of Angers. Conscious of the inexperience of the superior, yet unwilling to change her, Mother Euphrasia sent an older nun as assistant superior.

It didn't take long for frictions to develop between the two, and in due course they both appealed to Father Moreau. His decision was that the issues belonged to the internal administration of the community and that the Mother Superior's decision could not be challenged. Sister Stanislaus, the assistant superior, returned to Angers extremely bitter toward Father Moreau, whom she accused of having deceived her.

The incident would not merit mention were it not for its influence on a much more important problem that was coming to a head at that time. Mother Euphrasia, who had previously been superior of Tours, had founded Angers as a first step in a plan to bring all Good Shepherd convents under a central control. This would facilitate the changing of Sisters from one house to another according to need, make it easier to define and maintain common purposes, and remove obstacles to enforcing the rule which would always persist while each house was under direct control of the local Bishop.

The entire community of Angers was in full agreement with Mother Euphrasia, but they realized that opposition could be anticipated both from existing houses and from the bishops. The former would be reluctant to abdicate their relative autonomy under the general supervision of their respective bishops for the specific control of a superior located at a new house whose viewpoints had not even been tested by time. The latter would undoubtedly resist canonical exemption from their jurisdiction.

When Father Moreau approached the Angers convent with the request to make a foundation at Le Mans, the nuns decided that this should be the first step toward execution of their project. They, accordingly, drew up a document to be signed by the sisters who would go to Le Mans, pledging continued dependence on the mother house and the Bishop of Angers. But both the document and the intention were concealed from Father Moreau and from the Bishop of Le Mans.

During the following months, the nuns at Angers carried their intention several steps further. They drew up a plan to establish a generalate, to be located at Angers, and to have jurisdiction over all new foundations made by the Angers Sisters and (under certain conditions) existing Good Shepherd houses. The Bishop of Angers as ecclesiastical superior of the proposed mother house agreed. Rome, however, when asked approval in April 1833, the same month in which the Le Mans foundation was made, ruled a generalate could be created only if all existing Good Shepherd houses accepted.

Notwithstanding Rome's unfavorable decision, Mother Euphrasia and her associates continued to believe in the generalate, and the entire community made a vow to promote it in every possible way. Five months later, they signed a document which modified the constitution given by St. John Eudes to the nuns of the Good Shepherd by declaring (*Constitution 52*) that all convents founded or to be founded from Angers would recognize Angers as their mother house and its prioress as their superior. Their ecclesiastical superior under the authority of the Holy See would be the Bishop of Angers or a priest named by him.

In the meantime, the sisters both at Le Mans and Angers continued to be delighted with the help the new foundation was receiving from Father Moreau and were impressed by "the marvels he accomplished," as Mother Euphrasia summed up his work. It occurred to them that he might be the one to find a way to the goal of a generalate they so ardently desired.

They decided accordingly to enlist his aid, but without acquainting him with all the facts. They concealed the pledge taken before leaving Angers, as well as the subsequent modification of the Constitutions. Nor did they make any mention of the fact that they were also being advised by a former chaplain, a Father Perché. This young priest had been transferred by his Bishop to a parish at a distance from Angers, but he maintained regular contact with them and was fully informed of all their plans and actions.

Father Moreau thought that the idea of a generalate was excellent, for he was convinced that a central inspiration and direction of good works was an urgent need for the Church in France. He immediately wrote to Mother Euphrasia that one would have to be blind not to approve of her project, and he followed up his letter with an outline for a plan of action.

The document, containing the "Statutes for the Association for the Establishment of the Generalate in the Monastery of the Good Shepherd," reflects Father Moreau's usual systematic approach to a problem. He proposed an organization

> to assist by secret but effective means in obtaining from the Holy See the establishment of a generalate in the Monastery of the Good Shepherd at Angers, in order to ensure the good results of the Institute of Our Lady of Charity in all the communities of the order which may wish to join.

An expression of approval from existing Good Shepherd convents would count heavily with the Holy See, and at this point Father Moreau felt he could contribute positively. He was independently engaged in organizing an apostolic project of his own, a society or association of priests to be helpers in all good works. They could preach annual retreats in Good Shepherd convents and use the occasion to persuade bishops and local superiors of the advantages of the generalate.

For all future foundations, the superior and her council should bind themselves by vow to accept the generalate. The bishop should agree to send postulants to the Angers novitiate, and Angers would undertake not to keep subjects so sent.

The basic difference in Father Moreau's stand and that of the sisters emerges in a clause providing that the statutes of the proposed association should be approved by the bishop of Le Mans as well as the bishop of Angers. This shows that he thought of the Le Mans convent as under the exclusive jurisdiction of the Le Mans diocese until the bishop agreed to relax his authority over it.

Finally, the document specified that Father Moreau himself was to be asked "to accept the title and duties of superior of the present association."

The reaction of the Angers community to Father Moreau's suggestion that he should become superior makes it clear that he had not discussed this important point with them in advance. And even though he had no reason to suspect that they were totally committed to another candidate for the post, his blunt presentation of himself does seem strange. Perhaps what he had in mind was that Bishop Carron might look more favorably on the proposal if he were to be in control; and in his approach to the problem, the approval of the Bishop of Le Mans was essential to success.

Whatever the intention, the result was disastrous. At the very time the project reached Angers, Sister Stanislaus was bitterly denouncing to her companions and Father Perché the "trickery" of the man who had ousted her in disgrace from Le Mans. Here was proof that he was ambitious as well as tricky. As for his offer of help, his society of auxiliary priests existed only in his mind.

When Father Moreau went to Angers, his reception was polite but noncommittal. Mother Euphrasia and the community asked more time before deciding. In a subsequent account, he said the reactions had been favorable but that everything changed after he left. That impression may have been mistaken. His own guilelessness always influenced his dealings with people, making him interpret polite words as expressing approval. And he certainly was conscious of some currents of which he did not approve, for he commented on the tendency "to want to bypass Rome and set up the generalate temporarily with only the approval of the Bishop of Angers."

What he had no way of knowing was that this tendency had been formalized in *Constitution 52*, which was revealed only the following January through an indiscretion of Sister Stanislaus. About the same time, the Le Mans sisters showed it to Father Moreau. Perhaps to their surprise and certainly to their relief, he made no comment. He seems satisfied, they told Mother Euphrasia, who in turn informed Sister Stanislaus. They misinterpreted his silence. He was both surprised and pained. But he felt he should talk to the Bishop before expressing an opinion.

Bishop Carron had died in August, and Father Bouvier had been named to succeed but was not yet consecrated. Father Moreau decided to postpone consulting him, but someone else showed him *Constitution 52*, and his unfavorable reaction was immediate. This strikes me, he said, as "an infringement on the rights of the Holy See," referring not only to the recent decisions but also to the Bull of Benedict XIV approving the original constitutions, which forbade additions or changes.

He took no action, however, until the sisters themselves gave him a copy two weeks after his consecration, and even then he moved cautiously. Like Father Moreau, he thought the project intrinsically sound, but he wanted no involvement in canonical irregularities. He wrote Father Moreau, putting his reservations on record and urging him to straighten things out with all discretion.

In April 1834, accordingly, Father Moreau wrote Mother Euphrasia "under the seal of the most absolute secrecy," exposing his concern at length and enclosing the Bishop's letter. He wanted to promote the generalate, he said, promising never to trouble the union of the two houses at Angers and Le Mans and the dependence of the latter on the former. He added that he thought Bishop Bouvier would not take such an initiative unless circumstances forced his hand.

This letter is as tactful as it is generous. Father Moreau laid down no specific conditions, though it is quite clear that both the Bishop and he believed that *Constitution 52* should be withdrawn until approved by the Holy See. He simply urged that she and he must be in perfect agreement and that they should work together to keep differences from becoming public knowledge.

These details define Father Moreau's attitude. There is no rancor at the offhand rejection of his plan, no recrimination for failure to reveal information to which as ecclesiastical superior he had a right.

The letter, nevertheless, achieved none of the intended purposes, and that for a curious reason. Word had just reached Angers that powerful friends had intervened at Rome and that a favorable ruling by the Holy See was imminent. Bishop Bouvier's reservation and Father Moreau's objection hinged on possible infringement of Rome's rights. If Gregory XVI said yes, no need to worry about Benedict XIV's no a century earlier.

A new misunderstanding had also begun. As Father Moreau was writing the long letter he hoped would end all misunderstandings and achieve a perfect agreement, Mother Euphrasia was giving Sister Stanislaus a report from the assistant superior at Le Mans. Having noted that Father Moreau was zealous in procuring spiritual and temporal advantages, she added that he favored a generalate but with the mother house at Le Mans.

The basis for this statement is unknown. Father Moreau later wrote that he not only never expressed but never entertained such a view. However, the accuracy of the charge had ceased to be important. Read with his previous request to be named superior of the association he had proposed, and his current opposition to *Constitution 52*, it provided convincing evidence to the advocates of a generalate located at Angers that he was the protagonist in a subtle plot. Their conclusion was that, while hiding behind Bishop Bouvier, he was really instigating the Bishop to destroy them.

Late in May a further incident developed. A postulant sent from Le Mans to the Angers novitiate wrote Father Moreau that she felt strongly urged to make the vow of the generalate and also questioned the need to return to Le Mans for profession.

He replied that he would warmly approve a vow to promote the generalate, provided she added that she would seek this goal in conformity with canon law and the spirit of the institute. As regards returning for profession, he reminded her of an agreement made between Mother Euphrasia and himself when the house was established, that postulants would return to Le Mans when the ecclesiastical superior deemed it proper. He then asked her if she objected to coming to Le Mans at the end of her novitiate and if she was resolved to come for profession. Both questions were answered only with evasions.

Father Moreau now knew that Angers was determined to force the issue. He reminded Mother Euphrasia that "whoever has the office of ecclesiastical superior shall see to it that the Rule and Constitutions be carefully observed, and that no abuse, novelty or change be introduced." Having listed the changes introduced by *Constitution 52*, he laid down a series of stipulations for the Le Mans foundation, for which he alone was responsible. He requested an immediate written promise from the Angers council, signed by all its members, that novices from Le Mans would not have to take the vow in question before its approval by the Holy See, that before this approval no use would be made of Le Mans subjects or resources without his consent, that Le Mans novices at Angers would be inspired with sentiments of union, dependence, and devotion to their own house, and that all would come to Le Mans for profession.

The Angers council had made up its mind about Father Moreau and could see in these demands only the carping of frustrated ambition. Confident that Rome would soon reverse itself, it temporized with a succession of evasive replies. But Bishop Bouvier was not a man to trifle with. After an inconclusive visit to the convent and to the Bishop of Angers, he made his own decision, declaring the Le Mans convent to be autonomous, bound to that at Angers only by the bonds of charity and family relationship.

The reaction at Angers was as extreme as it was unedifying. A former novitiate companion wrote the young superioress at Le Mans:

> Perhaps you will object that the authority of my bishop and the correctness of his reasons, along with the uprightness of his views, make me inclined in his favor. This is all error, false inspiration, illusion, and a snare of the devil. For you, there is no light outside obedience to our bishop and our Mother—such is the Will of God.

Understandably enough, this letter found its way to Bishop Bouvier, who in turn sent it with a protest to the Bishop of Angers, thereby adding to the recriminations. Nor was obedience to their own bishop unquestioning. One sister refused him copies of *Constitution 52*, though (as she herself reported) she thought he was going to excommunicate her.

Father Perché was denounced to the chancery as the main instigator of the trouble, as apparently he was. Mother Euphrasia and her assistant were forbidden to write him. But even this did not break the lines of communication, for at the insistence of the sisters he came to consult with them. They had wanted him to visit secretly at the Angers convent, but he decided it would be more discreet to go to that of Poitiers.

The Bishop of Angers had never canonically released the sisters who had gone to Le Mans. This situation was now remedied, the Angers diocese renouncing jurisdiction over the religious at Le Mans who declared in writing their unwillingness to return. Despite Mother Euphrasia's efforts to persuade them, all but one chose to stay.

The separation of the two communities was permanent. Rome soon afterward authorized Angers to become the mother house of a new society, all future foundations to remain dependent, as Mother Euphrasia had wanted. From this source grew a major congregation with more than a hundred houses when the foundress died in 1868.

But Le Mans was not of their number. Outraged by the efforts of Angers to influence the sisters under his jurisdiction, Bishop Bouvier insisted on reorganizing it as a completely autonomous unit. Father Moreau remained ecclesiastical superior, and his untiring efforts produced excellent material and spiritual progress. In 1852, he obtained legal recognition for the house as a charitable foundation, thus relieving himself of personal responsibility for its financial administration. In 1858 he resigned as ecclesiastical superior. But even then he retained a constant interest in this first child of his charity, one for which his love was measured by the intensity of the birth pangs of suffering he had endured for it. More than a hundred years later, the convent still continues its good work at Le Mans under the name of the Community of Our Lady of Charity called Good Shepherd.

CHAPTER SIX

Holy Cross Takes Shape

By the time he had reached his middle thirties, Father Moreau had certainly become an important man in the church life of Le Mans. He was scripture professor, and, in January 1835, he was also appointed assistant superior of the major seminary. He was an honorary canon of the cathedral of Le Mans, that perfect expression of the soul of medieval France rivaling in beauty of architecture and sensitivity of decoration the better-known cathedral of nearby Chartres. He was the ecclesiastical superior of the Good Shepherd Convent, and even if he himself grieved at the greater promise that had not been fulfilled, what the public saw was the rapid growth and important social contribution of this recent foundation. Under his inspiration and direction, the Brothers of St. Joseph had been reborn, and their new mother house at Le Mans was attracting numerous novices.

Such was the man's physical and mental vigor that he not only handled all these assignments but gave such attention to each as almost to make it seem his sole concern. And he still found time to give missions and retreats, for which he was in great demand. Those who saw and heard him were immediately struck by his appearance, which was in keeping with the qualities of his soul.

He had a very high forehead with receding hair. His face was that of an ascetic—long, lean, controlled. But the eyes constituted his most striking feature. Eyes of fire, a contemporary called them. They held the audience and projected the dedication and determination of the preacher.

"One's first impression is that he is one of these peasant priests who are not worth very much, and this impression was not removed by hearing his Le Mans accent, which found expression in several everyday phrases." Such was the first reaction of the famous Catholic journalist Louis Veuillot when he met him a few years later. But he hastened to add that the first impression was deceptive. "After chatting with him for some time," he continued, "one sees that his eyes are very alert, his mind simple, firm, and resourceful, and his heart burning with love. He is an outstanding man and a saint. God has come to his aid in marvelous ways."

Notwithstanding so many achievements, Father Moreau was not satisfied. He was conscious of the weakness of his works, of their dependence on him. He needed a unifying organization that would provide inspiration, direction, and permanence for the others, while performing specific tasks of its own at the same time. And so he kept coming back in his own mind to the idea of a society of priests.

Several years earlier, he had outlined to his bishop an idea for an association of priests "well versed in both sacred and profane sciences, and capable of raising teaching standards in the seminaries and colleges of the diocese." This was in itself a vast program, but it fell short of Father Moreau's concept of the needs, and accordingly it was refined and expanded in a subsequent memorandum which called for an association of priests to include both teachers and missionaries.

Bishop Carron apparently approved, but he did not feel strongly enough on the subject to overrule objections raised by Father Bouvier, the seminary superior. We have already had some examples of the complicated relations which existed between

Father Bouvier and Father Moreau. The two men admired and respected each other, but they were poles apart on basic issues, and neither yielded easily. Their intransigence would cause much pain to both, but especially to Father Moreau, in the years to come, after Father Bouvier became bishop.

Whether their underlying differences influenced Father Bouvier's position on this occasion is not clear. It may well be that he believed the seminary needed Father Moreau and that the success of this project would take him away from it. In any case, Bishop Carron limited himself to authorizing Father Moreau to send three young clerics, at his own expense, to study at the Sorbonne and obtain university diplomas.

Though the concession may seem slight, it was in fact quite substantial. Sending these students to the Sorbonne ranged Father Moreau publicly on the "progressive" side in a bitterly controversial issue. For he was proclaiming that Catholic education must incorporate the best elements of the secular system, that the schools he hoped to establish could attract top students only if the teachers were fully qualified. Later, he would apply the same principle for the Brothers of St. Joseph, insisting that they spare no effort to get state diplomas.

Even on this point Father Bouvier was in disagreement, and one of his first acts as bishop was to recall the students from the Sorbonne. Father Moreau's response illustrates very well his spirit of obedience. In addition to being a spiritual man, he was a theologian and a canonist. When a superior made a decision, he accepted it. But he did not necessarily feel bound by a superior's expressed preference, if he believed the superior mistaken. And he also saw the possibility of a superior later reversing himself. This was his attitude toward the Angers sisters. You must obey Rome's ruling, he insisted, though you can continue to work and pray to have it changed.

Such was his attitude now. Accepting the bishop's ruling without protest, he nevertheless began to develop a far more ambitious plan along the lines of the former one.

The idea which then began to unfold was of tremendous importance in relation to Father Moreau's lifework, for it reveals the kind of thinking that would produce the Congregation of Holy Cross. Strangely enough, it is not easy to determine who was author of the idea, and perhaps Father Moreau and his companions would not consider the question very important. Perhaps it has little meaning. Given a certain intellectual atmosphere and social conditions, many people think along parallel lines. What is important is a practical man with the mind of a visionary who can grasp the ideas and translate them into reality. Father Moreau was such a man.

As long ago as 1823, when Father Moreau and Father Dujarié first met, the two had discussed the possibility of forming an association of diocesan missionaries, with Father Dujarié as its head and Father Moreau as a member. In 1827, when Father Dujarié and Father Deshayes were working out a plan to fuse their respective teaching associations, they drafted an agreement in which they stated that both of them had long been of the opinion that an ecclesiastical superior was necessary for their groups of brothers and sisters. "But we have also felt," they continued,

> that to fill this office, the superior would have to be imbued with the spirit proper to these new societies, and that, consequently, he would have to be formed within them. We have thought that a society of five or six priests would surely be enough to guide us toward the desired goal. From its ranks would be chosen a superior of the three congregations.

The one who now put a similar project on paper was Brother André of the Brothers of St. Joseph, who was cooperating closely in the brothers' reform. And even after Father Moreau assumed the functions of superior of the institute, he kept in the background as much as possible, perhaps because of the unpleasant experience he had just had with the Good Shepherd convents.

As previously mentioned, Brother André, in November 1834, sent Bishop Bouvier a confidential letter asking him to investigate abuses and institute a reform. With it went a memorandum, which had also been approved by Father Moreau, and which incorporates many elements of his known thinking.

The memorandum envisaged the establishment of a vast institute with three branches, one of priests under the title of the Sacred Heart, a second of teaching brothers (the existing society), and a third of lay teachers called "Sons of Mary." The priests would be superiors of the institute, assuring enlightened and reliable government. They would direct the novitiate for the brothers and a teacher training college for the lay teachers. They would conduct their own boarding schools or colleges, and finally they would act as diocesan missionaries.

Bishop Bouvier made no immediate decision on this grandiose plan, contenting himself with approving the concrete steps being taken to reorganize the Brothers of St. Joseph. The idea of the three societies in one was, nevertheless, to stay with Father Moreau, as was the symbolism mentioned in Brother André's memorandum dedicating the three branches respectively to Jesus, Mary, and Joseph in the Holy Family, and also to the three persons of the Holy Trinity.

A little later, in June 1835, Father Moreau and the bishop had a talk, which Father Moreau immediately afterward summarized in a letter requesting specific decisions. The bishop eliminated the teaching function of the proposed society of priests. He also eliminated the society of lay teachers. What remained was an organization consisting of the Brothers of St. Joseph and a house of diocesan missionaries, which could also constitute a home for retired priests and a center for lay retreats.

Father Mollevaut, still active as Father Moreau's adviser, was delighted with the news. He wrote him several letters in which he sketched with prophetic foresight the path to follow and the goal to seek. There was no mention of a religious congregation in the canonical sense, but everything was being readied for it.

Choose young men at the end of their seminary course, when they are easiest to form, but preferring above all docility and good character, he told Father Moreau. If you take in sick or old priests, keep them apart, or you can never enforce the rule. Form the novices in habits of recollection, prayer, abnegation, humility, obedience, and patience. For the rest, "you can find everything in the life of St. Vincent de Paul, which is a handbook for all missionaries and all good priests."

The advice is eminently sound. The flowery presentation is understandable when one recalls that the words were written at the height of the Romantic period in literature. The same romantic attitude influenced all of life, and Father Moreau's steps after getting the bishop's approval reflect it. With his first four companions, two priests and two seminarians, he went in 1835 to the Trappist monastery of Port du Salut to make a retreat and inaugurate the association. He knew this solitude well, the abbot being a former fellow student at St. Sulpice.

They called themselves "auxiliary priests" to indicate that they would act as substitutes and occasional helpers, in addition to preaching missions in parishes. They agreed to live temporarily at St. Vincent's seminary, there to prepare under Father Moreau for their new life.

The first months were devoted principally to study, prayer, and the exercises of a holy life. Thanks to the free quarters at St. Vincent's Seminary, a small subsidy from Bishop Bouvier, and Father Moreau's salary as professor, the immediate living needs of all created no problem. Each day the group assembled in Father Moreau's room for an hour's meditation, particular examen, and spiritual reading. There were two weekly conferences, one on scripture and the other on moral theology. Topics were chosen and studied with a view to the needs of a new type of ministry.

The bishop had approved the plan for an organization to combine the Auxiliary Priests and the Brothers of St. Joseph, but Father Moreau knew that much still remained to be done before the idea could be made a reality. In particular, it was not going to be easy to develop among the brothers an understanding that their own future required such a development.

Things were starting to look up for the brothers. The new mother house and novitiate at Le Mans had ten brothers and nine novices, with fifty brothers dispersed in twenty-five schools. Their poverty was extreme, but fortunately the Good Shepherd convent was able and willing to meet their immediate needs, leaving Father Moreau free to concentrate on restoration of the religious spirit.

He had long admired the work of the teaching brothers established in neighboring dioceses by Father Jean Marie de Lamennais, the philosopher's brother, and he now went to seek his advice and study his organization, establishing a lifetime friendship and exchange of aid. Father Dujarié's original rule had been adopted from this same source. From his visit Father Moreau brought back great inspiration. Particularly, it confirmed his conviction that the permanence of the society and spiritual progress of the members would best be guaranteed by religious vows.

Only a vow of obedience still held the members, and that for a year at a time. Many brothers objected to further obligations, an attitude strengthened by the widespread resistance to restoring or creating religious orders. Some theologians actually held that vows of religion taken by Frenchmen were void because of the civil law prohibitions. Father Moreau certainly did not share that view, nor did Father Lamennais, but its existence indicated the need for caution. Nevertheless, Father Moreau pressed onward, sowing the seed now in one mind, now in another.

Just when everything seemed to be moving along nicely, catastrophe struck in October 1836. Bishop Bouvier removed Father Moreau as scripture professor and assistant superior at the seminary. It is true that he had more than enough other work to occupy him, and some time earlier he had asked the bishop to be relieved of his classes. Apparently, however, this was not what motivated the move, nor was it so interpreted. As had happened before and would happen again, the bishop seems rather to have let his deep inner conflicts with Father Moreau build up to explosion point and turn into a rebuke what need only have been a decision of prudent administration.

Some of Father Moreau's anguish emerges in a letter pouring out his soul with customary frankness to Father Mollevaut. Seeing himself publicly represented as having lost his bishop's confidence, he feared that all his foundations were threatened. Nevertheless, he decided that the Auxiliary Priests must immediately leave the seminary, though without money or a place to spend the next night. He was ready for the worst. "If this brings us nothing but a great public humiliation, we will go off to hide in La Trappe and there prepare for eternity."

The next day, a friend found him a room for himself. The following morning, after Mass in the cathedral, a man known for his hostility to the Church offered him at a low rent a big house suitable for his group of priests. He accepted immediately. Then he took his companions to La Trappe for another retreat while their new home was made ready. Here they prayed, meditated, and made a first draft of their rule.

Bishop Bouvier not only approved the rule but wrote Father Moreau a gracious letter expressing infinite gratitude to him for starting this work. To give substance to his words, he promised an annual subsidy of two thousand francs, more than enough to pay their rent. These generous gestures are hard to reconcile with the churlishness of the ejection from the seminary a few months earlier, but there are several such inexplicable incidents in the relations of these two extraordinary men.

Earlier the bishop had excluded teaching from the activities of the Auxiliary Priests, but he now yielded on this point also. They were ten in number when they occupied their rented home late in 1836, and they started classes in temporary quarters while awaiting completion of a school on the nearby property of the Brothers of St. Joseph.

Everything looked fine, if only they could find money for food. Hunger would always be a limiting factor in Father

Moreau's activities. The Church in France had been stripped of its resources. The wealthy members of the community were usually those farthest from religious practice. The common people were impoverished by runaway inflation, which began with the Napoleonic Wars and persisted through the century. They were lucky when they could meet their most urgent needs.

Such also was the condition of Father Moreau and his companions. Poverty shines through his letters. It can be glimpsed in the fears of those around him whose faith in providence was weaker than his. Do not take on new obligations, they constantly urged, when you can't meet your existing ones.

But that didn't frighten him. It was the only existence he had ever known. His parents had survived it, and their parents before them. If the immediate family had nothing, there was always the wider family of the village. Nobody ever starved to death.

And so we are back to the family which looms so large in Father Moreau's concept of organization and gives Holy Cross its distinctive spirit. When the brothers arrived from Ruillé, he got the Good Shepherd sisters to feed them. Now the brothers were getting on their feet. They could carry the Auxiliary Priests for a while.

Such was Father Moreau's logic, but not all the brothers went along. They were scarcely making ends meet, they said. They would be ruined under the additional load. That was what they said, but some of them had a deeper reason. They did not want priests as superiors.

Father Moreau felt that time would achieve the union of the two groups which both he and Father Dujarié believed was essential to the expansion of the brothers. He saw, however, that it was necessary to resolve a dispute over property that could prejudice the decision. He accordingly assembled the priests and brothers and made an accounting of the assets of the Brothers of St. Joseph, which totaled twenty-five thousand francs. These assets, he proposed, should go in a common treasury, and if they ever separated the brothers would get a credit in the division. As security, he offered his own property already occupied by the brothers. The agreement was formalized in a Fundamental Pact signed by all the Brothers of St. Joseph and the Auxiliary Priests, numbering about fifty and ten respectively, on March 1, 1837. It was a major step toward the full union of the two societies in the Congregation of Holy Cross.

To supplement the income from teaching and missions, Father Moreau formed the Associates of St. Joseph, and this organization proved as successful as the Associates of the Good Shepherd who provided a regular income for the orphanage. As the work developed, it was expanded to include distinguished patrons. At critical moments, it was able to influence public opinion and save the schools each time a revolutionary outbreak threatened them.

Two years after Bishop Bouvier had approved a rule for the Auxiliary Priests, Father Moreau submitted a draft constitution for the Brothers of St. Joseph. This document incorporated the fruit of much reflection and discussion, for he had now been their superior for six years.

Teaching on the primary level was to be the specific function of the institute, and it would be composed of men who did not aspire to the priesthood. The rules directed periods of daily prayer and spiritual reading, described the habit to be worn, and regulated details of personal appearance. The brothers, for example, were forbidden to wear sideburns.

The bishop approved the provisions concerning internal discipline and the founding of the schools. But he thought that the rules dealing with the government of the society and the spiritual life of the members tended to push the institute too much to the status of a religious order. He therefore directed that they should undergo a trial period before being put into final form.

While the membership remained small, it was comparatively easy to bring everyone together to consider a problem, as Father Moreau had done in the disputes over financial relations of priests and brothers. Growth would, however, soon make this system impractical, and, accordingly, provision was made for a periodic general chapter in which delegates of all the members would meet to elect the superior general and other high superiors and to make decisions affecting the society as a whole. The Constitutions of Holy Cross, as approved by the Holy See in 1857, declared specifically that the final authority in the congregation was vested in the general chapter, so that it even outranked the superior general, a point which later assumed importance when disputes developed between Father Moreau and some of his subordinates. The Holy Cross system also developed provincial chapters, with advisory, supervisory, and legislative authority in matters pertaining to each province, and local chapters with similar powers in each community.

The new constitutions brought rapid progress. Father Moreau was proving an inspired leader, and experience was refining his techniques. Perhaps most striking of these was clarity of purpose combined with openness of method. Once he fixed a goal, he moved toward it against every obstacle. Nevertheless, he tried neither to deceive nor to crush opposition. He had an admirable, almost naive, confidence in the inevitability of the triumph of right and truth. Once the correctness of a course of action was clear, he went ahead. It was a technique that would win many victories but also cause many misunderstandings and sufferings.

A successful application occurred at this time. Despite the evident progress, Father Moreau knew that some brothers remained unhappy about the economics of their relationship with the Auxiliary Priests. Instead of silencing them, as was his right in view of the recent unanimous decision, not to mention his moral and legal status as superior, he made a new financial accounting which showed that the priests were more than paying their way. It was agreed to create a full community of assets.

With equal forthrightness he fought for the teaching rights he considered essential for the new mother house. Here, too, he achieved his objectives, but a series of clashes left scars that did not quickly heal.

The clashes occurred with the civil authorities over the brothers' novitiate and mother house at Le Mans. Father Moreau presented a petition to the Education Minister in Paris for a small subsidy, but the district school board and the prefect of the Department, the approval of both of whom was necessary, objected on the ground that the novitiate had been moved from Ruillé to Le Mans without authorization. After much negotiation and discussion, the Minister ruled that Father Moreau had been entirely within his rights in moving the headquarters of the institute.

Very soon, however, a proposal to transfer the boarding school from Ruillé to Le Mans provoked a new storm. The prefect was still resentful because of his recent defeat, and he refused to go along with the other local officials, who were willing to approve. Once again, Father Moreau appealed directly to the Minister and succeeded in getting his agreement. This enabled him to open the school on time in temporary quarters.

Thirteen months later, however, when they were ready to transfer to the permanent buildings just a few yards from the temporary ones, a new crisis occurred. The sanitary inspector and the doctor appointed by the local school board to examine the premises said they were too damp and would need a year to dry out. Father Moreau submitted evidence to the contrary, then moved right in without waiting for the board to reverse itself. Such high-handedness added to the bitterness of the opposition. The board, nevertheless, decided to bide its time rather than move against so formidable an adversary on a technicality.

Within a short time of the transfer from Ruillé, the school at Le Mans showed signs of developing into an important educational center. While the rapid progress was gratifying, it was not without its dangers. The State was jealous of any competition. Because it was unable to provide schools for all, it tolerated private institutions. But when a private school established such standards of excellence as to draw students from State schools, an outcry would develop.

Such a situation began to arise. The local prefect attacked not only Father Moreau and the Brothers of St. Joseph, but also the minor seminary of the diocese. However, the plan backfired when Bishop Bouvier became incensed and brought the matter to higher authority, protesting against "the spirit of Voltaire which dominates the middle classes and the government officials." The education ministry in Paris approved the brothers and even asked for some of them to teach in overseas French territories. Father Moreau was not ready to undertake this venture, but he seized the opportunity of pushing ahead more rapidly with his plans for a primary boarding school. Though the prefect continued his opposition, Father Moreau persisted and finally won the required authorizations.

Father Moreau's next objective was a secondary school, a project subject to extreme complications. The almost total monopoly of secondary education established under Napoleon still remained. Specifically, two obstacles had to be surmounted. One was the law debarring a teacher who refused to depose that he was not a member of an unauthorized congregation. The other was that, where a public secondary school existed, a private institution might teach only elementary subjects not included in the government school curriculum, or repeat the government school courses, for which pupils got no credit unless they attended them also in the government school.

The possibility of administrative discretion always existed, but Father Moreau's relations with the school board were against him. It happened, however, that in 1838 he and two associates, while preaching in a neighboring district, persuaded the mayor to return to the practice of his religion, after an absence of thirty years. The mayor in gratitude used his influence with high-placed friends, and a decree of authorization arrived from Paris before the local people even knew what was happening.

There was an uproar. The civil authorities, let down by their own chiefs, protested to the bishop. As spokesman they found a priest who preferred a state monopoly in education to the academic freedom on which Father Moreau rested his case. Bishop Bouvier, though sympathetic to the rights of the civil power, did not support so extreme a position. But he wanted friendly relations with the local authorities, and he tried to dissuade Father Moreau from proceeding with his plans.

At the first opportunity Bishop Bouvier asked if it was true that Father Moreau planned to teach Latin in his new school. Latin was the touchstone. It marked the intention to pass from primary to secondary studies. "Not only Latin, Excellency," Father Moreau answered with more directness than tact, "but Greek and Hebrew, if God wills."

"I don't like the plan, and I have promised to oppose it," the bishop replied with equal directness. If they persisted, he added, he would never again set foot in the community.

Father Moreau was distressed. He considered the secondary school essential to development of the enterprise and suspected that the bishop's opposition was to himself personally rather than to the project. His reaction was that he ought to resign as superior for the sake of the work. But when he consulted his spiritual director, Father Mollevaut, he was told he should not dream of resigning and should continue with his plans unless the bishop formally forbade him. This the bishop was not prepared to do. Nevertheless, a residue of unpleasantness remained, and it was in fact a very long time before His Excellency revisited in Father Moreau's little community.

As this incident once more demonstrates, relations between Father Moreau and his bishop were not improving with the passage of time. Here were two men who were extremely alike in temperament and purpose, yet they could never agree for long on the methods to be used in order to reach the end they both sought to achieve. It is, therefore, not only appropriate but necessary to examine the causes of their conflicts. This in turn requires a quick review of Bishop Bouvier's own background.

The future bishop of Le Mans was born in 1783, before the Revolution had reached the height of its fury. His father was a village carpenter, and John Baptist was apprenticed in his early teens to the same trade. His studies posed even greater problems than those of Basil Moreau, problems not only of money but of human drama. They were conducted in large part in secret by fugitive priests.

The background helps to explain the character of the man—determined, difficult, quick to elevate a detail to the status of principle, yet behind it all ready to bow to authority and humble himself in submission. What it does not explain is his learning.

As a student he had exchanged pledges with a companion to form a mission band to evangelize the countryside. His bishop refused to approve, sending him instead to teach, and soon he was acquiring a reputation as a philosopher and a theologian. He started to publish his courses, then to assemble them in a textbook embracing the entire range of seminary studies of philosophy, dogma, and moral theology. It was so much better than the old text used by generations of clerics, including Basil Moreau and himself, that it was quickly adopted by most French seminaries, running through fifteen editions between 1834 and 1858.

He was superior of St. Vincent's Seminary where he earned the respect and affection of Basil Moreau the student. He, for his part, considered Basil an outstanding student and model seminarian, for he recommended him for the graduate studies which would bring him back to St. Vincent's as a professor and assistant superior.

Neither could, however, for long overlook their differences. These began in philosophy, where Father Bouvier was a Cartesian while Father Moreau followed Lamennais, though not so wholeheartedly as did other members of the seminary faculty. Moral theology created no problems, for Bouvier was an antirigorist, and his writings were instrumental in restoring St. Alphonsus Liguori to favor in French classrooms. It was in dogma that the issue was really joined.

Bouvier was less extreme in his Gallicanism than many earlier French churchmen. He was quick, for example, to challenge the infringement of the rights of the Holy See involved in the attempt of the Good Shepherd sisters of Angers to change the approved constitutions on their own initiative. But he held for a broad autonomy of the French Church and even questioned the validity of canon law at variance with the civil law. Emotions were deeply involved in this area. Dom Guéranger, Abbot of Solesmes, became recognized as leader of the Roman faction, and his conflicts with Bishop Bouvier had so many ramifications that he was even accused of denouncing the bishop's theological works to the Holy Office. Father Moreau was never one to hide his stand, and he made no secret either of his intellectual support of or personal friendship with Dom Guéranger.

At the same time, Bouvier and Moreau shared a common concept of the apostolate and a like zeal for souls. Obedience had prevented Bouvier from following his youthful wish to form a missionary association, but his concentration on teaching and writing did not lessen his zeal for the active apostolate. His strong stand determined the decision in 1818 to form an institute of teaching brothers for the diocese of Le Mans. It was he who persuaded Father Dujarié to undertake the work. He figures in the list of early contributors, and he not only helped design the habit to be worn by the brothers, but he also paid the bill for the first two delivered by the tailor. Both before and after becoming bishop of Le Mans, he was convinced of the value of the Brothers of St. Joseph and backed all Father Dujarié's initiatives, including his proposals to form an association of missionary priests and his later decision to abdicate in favor of Father Moreau.

Where he drew the line was at the point of escaping the bishop's jurisdiction. He was not a man to trifle with, and it may well be that his insistence on the rights of bishops might have been less firm if he was not himself one. Nevertheless, his basic position was one of clear principle flowing from his Gallicanism. The record entitles him to be credited with good faith.

Accordingly, although he resented Father Moreau's support as a professor of views conflicting with his own, he backed him in his other activities. The two maintained a perfect understanding in the entire Good Shepherd controversy. The bishop stood equally with Father Moreau when he took charge of the Brothers of St. Joseph, as long as he was content to follow the previous pattern of organization. He similarly went along with his plan to start an association of missionary priests. It was only when Father Moreau sought to introduce basic changes into these groups, changes which Bishop Bouvier correctly anticipated would transform them into religious congregations directly dependent on the Holy See and thus exempt from the control of the bishop, that the opposition developed.

With hindsight we can say with some assurance that Father Moreau was right and the bishop wrong. But the bishop had to make a prudential judgment in concrete circumstances, and, even leaving aside his theological resistance to expansion of Rome's area of action, his decision cannot be rejected offhand. His specific job was to ensure the spiritual wellbeing of his diocese, and he was under the extreme pressures of abnormal need and a shortage of helpers. Was it unreasonable of him to oppose a move which threatened to remove from his jurisdiction his only teachers and some of his most apostolic priests?

The issues were legitimate, but unfortunately in human affairs secondary aspects tend to compound differences. To defend a position, it becomes strategically useful to establish converging protective points, and soon one forgets which is the essential and which the ancillary. For example, people who opposed Father Moreau for entirely different reasons played on the bishop's suspicions for their own ends. His support of a Good Shepherd postulant who insisted on staying in the convent against the wishes of her influential parents made an enemy of Father Dubois, the vicar-general. Father Moreau was accused of shifting position and using underhanded tactics. When a few months later one of the Auxiliary Priests submitted a series of complaints against Father Moreau's government, the bishop was conditioned to take him seriously.

A more diplomatic man might have anticipated and avoided such incidents. But Father Moreau was of Le Mans. Like his forebears he just went on doing what he believed right. What could be more infuriating?

When Father Heurtebize, a former fellow professor and now superior at St. Vincent's, was demoted for the outrage of carrying to Rome an appeal against the bishop's ruling and winning his case there, Father Moreau invited him to join Holy Cross as novice master. It was an extreme instance of his lack of tact. But it was not an isolated one. He equally refused to stop pestering the bishop on a subject on which he should have recognized no common ground existed, the status of the "pious girls" who kept house at Holy Cross.

And so the clash of these two mighty warriors of the Lord built up and up with the hopelessness of a Greek tragedy. Even Pius IX had only one solution. Bishops do not live forever, he one day consoled Father Moreau. It was true. Death finally opened for Father Moreau the way to the goals the bishop had opposed. But the wounds continued to fester and suppurate for years.

CHAPTER SEVEN

Assembly at Sainte-Croix

The unceremonious termination of his activities as a professor described in the last chapter marked the parting of the ways for Father Moreau. It had been the intention of his superiors, when they sent him for higher studies to St. Sulpice, that he would in due course become superior of the seminary and spend his life in that post. It was not what he himself would have chosen, but he accepted his assignment and performed it thoroughly and faithfully. In less than ten years from his appointment to St. Vincent's, he had become assistant superior.

Now all that was changed. Henceforth, his primary function would be to direct the other forces he had set in motion, to lead them step by step to the full status of a religious congregation with a worldwide scope and mission.

At the moment, there was little to indicate such a development. If the dream had already taken shape in the founder's heart, he kept it hidden there. Reality was much more modest. It consisted of two small groups organized to serve the bishop of Le Mans, men with little understanding of their common purpose and able to break away almost at will.

The brothers had been installed since 1835 in a house in the borough of Sainte-Croix, which was identified on old maps as Notre Dame. The name seemed just right to Father Moreau, Notre Dame de Sainte-Croix, Our Lady of Holy Cross. That was what he would call the mother house. In due course, when the priests moved in, they became known as the Fathers of Holy Cross. That suited him too. When the group should need an official title, it would be the Congregation of Holy Cross.

The property was in his own name, and it had come to him in a way that helps to explain the kind of man he was. While at St. Sulpice, he had met an old priest named de Lisle who was such a victim of scruples that for fifteen years he could not say Mass. Each day he began his breviary several times but never could complete it.

Father de Lisle lived at Le Mans with a fellow priest, with whom he had shared exile in England and Germany during the Terror. When Father Moreau came as professor to St. Vincent's, he began to visit him each day and say his office with him, forcing him to keep in step. He gradually imposed his own peace of mind on the old man and, acting as his assistant, got him to say Mass again.

Father de Lisle, in 1832, expressed his gratitude by giving Father Moreau some property he owned, reserving the right to use it during his lifetime. The deed described it as "consisting of a main house with yard and garden, buildings for the residence of the caretaker and the garden tools, with property covering somewhat more than seven acres." Its value was about 20,000 francs. Such holdings, used partly for pleasure and partly to produce income, were frequent on the outskirts of small French towns. They usually consisted of a small farm with a house where the owner spent the summer or the wine-making season.

The location had traditions to commend it to Father Moreau. The parish of Sainte-Croix had grown up around a church built by St. Bernard, a sixth-century bishop of Le Mans, as a hospice for pilgrims. The church was torn down during the Revolution and the parish absorbed into a neighboring one. The borough, nevertheless, retained a separate civil administration. It was a community of farm homes set in fields and vineyards, but the city was growing toward it. Soon, a residential section would surround the de Lisle property.

When, in 1835, Father Moreau needed a place near Le Mans for the Brothers of St. Joseph, his friend agreed immediately to waive his life estate.

The farmhouse became the residence. On November 1, after a minimum of remodeling, the official installation took place. The quarters were very cramped, but it was agreed that they would have to do for the present and that whatever funds were available should be devoted to a school building. Even a year later, when the Auxiliary Priests had to leave the seminary, there was no question of accommodating them. They had to move to a rented house.

It was, nevertheless, still Father Moreau's intention to unite the two groups both physically and spiritually at the earliest opportunity. The number of Auxiliary Priests soon grew to ten, making it possible for him to develop what was his second purpose in founding them. While some continued to give missions, he set several aside to begin a boarding school, at first in the rented house. Soon a new building was constructed on the Sainte-Croix property, and the two branches were physically joined.

It was a time of intense activity, of many trials and visible progress. While the school was being organized, the attention of the public was aroused by the missions and retreats, which were crowned by extraordinary results. Father Moreau himself led the mission band and usually preached the opening and closing sermons, following the model of the Society for the Missions of France, which for twenty-five years had been reviving religion throughout the country.

The technique was spectacular. Descending on a town, the missionaries set themselves to win attention by impressive ceremonies. There were open-air sermons, dialogue instructions, public processions, erections of Calvaries. A favorite Moreau ceremony was to install the Way of the Cross, a devotion then becoming popular. One of his first requests from the pope, when they became friends, was the faculty for all his priests to do so.

These missions produced a real awakening of religious fervor. Crowds flocked to sermons and services and received the sacraments. Conversions testified to the value of the methods and the zeal of the preachers. These evident results in turn impacted the missionaries and spurred them to greater efforts of personal sanctification.

Events were thus conspiring with Father Moreau's long cherished ambition to move ever closer to the life of perfection as traditionally practiced in the Church. He had himself long felt called to the religious state, having been dissuaded by his spiritual director from joining the Trappists, and later the Sulpicians. He had also become convinced that the permanence and spiritual development of the Brothers of St. Joseph could be assured only with vows. By the bishop's decision, each brother was free to take vows or not, as he chose, but many had done so. To Father Moreau it seemed logical that a religious superior should himself be a religious. The time had come for another decisive step.

He outlined his thinking in a circular letter dated January 1, 1840. The working association of the brothers and priests should evolve into a single congregation at Holy Cross. He proposed shortly, he told them, to follow the example of the brothers who had taken vows and to open a novitiate for the Auxiliary Priests.

"I have decided to make the vows of poverty and obedience," he wrote, "as much to edify the Auxiliary Priests as to give an example to the brothers, . . . whose superior I could not continue to be if I did not walk at the head of the community."

Bishop Bouvier kept his reservations about some aspects of the work, and specifically about the gradual transformation into a religious congregation. But he was an honorable man, as a report to the Holy See in May 1840 demonstrates.

Father Moreau's community, he told the pope, was one of the most encouraging developments in the diocese. He stressed the zeal and rapid growth, reporting that they were now eighty-six persons in thirty-nine houses, and that a priest and several brothers had recently gone to Algeria, while others would soon leave for America. The pope for his part expressed satisfaction and hoped the good work would thrive. It was a fair augury.

The tug-of-war with the bishop nevertheless continued. Some priests did not want vows. They felt that the present organization was adequate for their purposes and that further sacrifice should not be imposed. Beneath the surface, too, smoldered the resistance of the French diocesan clergy to religious congregations.

The bishop's sentiments were on this side, while those of Father Mollevaut, Father Moreau's spiritual director, were even more strongly on the other. Father Mollevaut's ability to sweep away all the confusing accidental elements in a situation, to see not what was but what could and should be, to analyze the temporal in the light of the eternal—these qualities played an incalculable part in leading Father Moreau to the goal he finally reached.

Strong in the support of his spiritual director, Father Moreau decided to force the issue with his unwilling bishop. And now, considering his spirit of obedience, one must define terms precisely. Both Father Mollevaut and he were good theologians, as was the bishop. They dealt with each other as professional men, making and assuming the necessary distinctions. They thought and spoke as theologians. When given an order by competent authority, Father Moreau obeyed blindly. But if a serious doubt existed as to the intention of his superior, and this is a question of fact to be judged by all the circumstances and not simply by the expressed words, he would not take refuge under the mantle of obedience. He was bound to do what he believed right. And if the competent authority was unwilling, as Bishop Bouvier frequently was, to assume responsibility by giving a formal command,

Father Moreau decided according to his own conscience even though he knew the superior was of a different opinion.

Such a situation now developed. He persisted in his request for permission to set up the novitiate for the priests and to take vows himself, and the bishop went along without enthusiasm. But once his hand was forced, he did have the generosity to officiate at the function on August 15, 1840, when Father Moreau and four Auxiliary Priests pronounced religious vows.

For Father Mollevaut this represented the fruit of years of guidance, and he came the following month to see the novitiate established in its own building near the principal house, with Father Moreau as novice master. He liked what he saw. He was delighted, he wrote on his return, to notice how easily the novices laughed, for it revealed their interior joy. He praised the progress Father Moreau had made in developing a kindly and mild character and urged him to have no fear of exaggerating in this direction.

The harmony was short-lived. New conflicts developed with the bishop, trivial in themselves but cumulatively serious. One concerned the postulant already mentioned who had entered the Good Shepherd convent against her parents' wishes. They were people of standing, and the bishop wanted to avoid friction. She is entitled to make her own decision, Father Moreau insisted, and he refused to use his authority as superior of the convent without a formal command from the bishop. The latter backed down but was very annoyed.

In this bad mood, the Bishop was ready to listen to complaints. Because they would not take vows, some of the Auxiliary Priests said, they were treated as second-class members of the community. They were forced to live as religious, and Father Moreau denied their right to choose their confessor and spiritual director.

The formal inquiry that resulted had its bright side, however. The bishop ordered each priest and brother to report in writing, and the documentation throws valuable sidelights on the way of life, while establishing the paucity of the dissidents. Many statements are fervent defenses of Father Moreau, who was always slow to defend himself, and they testify to his tremendous personal magnetism.

The inquiry proved the complaints unfounded. Specifically, it showed that all priests had faculties to hear confessions and that each was free to confess to any of the others. Each was also free to choose his spiritual director, though a periodic accounting of dispositions had to be made to the superior.

One strange charge raised a point that would recur. Father Moreau was said to have only younger priests and brothers on his council so that he could dominate them and turn the council into a rubber stamp of his own will. The criticism was shown to be unfair in this instance, but there is no doubt that Father Moreau was a strong personality. He was, however, aware of this and worked unceasingly to control his personal drives and to lead his companions only in directions in which he had first persuaded them they ought to go.

If anything, he tended to legalism in these matters. He was ready, for example, to give a detailed accounting of money trans-actions and to quote the precise regulation or constitution on which he based a stand. If, as was more than once charged, he had frequently to invoke formal obedience against a recalcitrant, he was deeply provoked before he did so. One problem inher-ited with the brothers was that many of them had little religious training. It was part of the tragedy of the times. The needs were so acute that they created a constant temptation to rush. Mother Euphrasia had yielded to this temptation when selecting the founding group for the Le Mans Good Shepherd convent. And Father Moreau was frequently to place in authority men with lit-tle understanding of religious obedience. In such circumstances, a superior had to remind a subject of the obligation of his vow far oftener than now occurs.

Father Champeau, a priest who played a major part in the development of the Congregation, showed a very deep under-standing of Father Moreau's character in his comments to Bishop

Bouvier. "In the general administration of the house, in his out-side contacts, and perhaps even in his dealings with you, your Lordship," Father Champeau wrote,

> he may have shown himself firm and unyielding on more than one occasion. Has he always been in the right? That is not my business. I feel, however, that without this energetic trait of character, he would never have accomplished all he has done. But this I say, and this I affirm, that with his priests in com-munity life he acts as a father. I have on many occa-sions admired the calmness and the moderation with which a man of his temperament, overwhelmed with work, bothered on all sides, and carrying on only by force of sheer energy, has put up with contradictions which were well calculated to give rise to irritation.

Housekeeping is always a time-consuming part of community life, and Father Moreau decided at an early date that he wanted sisters to assist with this work. He made several unsuccessful attempts at enlisting a community, in the meantime employing charwomen under his own sister and one of the Brothers of St. Joseph. This soon became a big operation, for they served the boarding school as well as the mother house and novitiate.

Understandably, girls of good moral background and pious life were selected, and it soon occurred to Father Moreau to form a religious community that could provide domestic service for Holy Cross. Bishop Bouvier did not like the idea; consequently the original constitution makes no mention of sisters, but only of priests and brothers. Father Moreau decided, nevertheless, to go ahead on an experimental basis, as he had done with the Auxil-iary Priests. The Superior of the Good Shepherd convent under-took to train postulants, and three were installed with her in 1841, where they were soon joined by a young lady who would become the first head of the sisters as Mary of the Seven Dolors. She was Léocadie Gascoin, a doctor's daughter.

Father Moreau took as much interest in them as in his other associates, giving frequent conferences in which he spoke in terms related to their own life and experiences while stressing their equal status with the members of the other branches of Holy Cross. He went to the convent each Sunday to get a report on the way they were observing the rule. He then gave a conference on their duties and offered practical suggestions to each on how to do her assigned work. He also arranged for the sisters to go each week for some hours to the Good Shepherd convent to talk to the prioress and get her advice on their spiritual progress, a practice that continued for several years.

Despite the lowly functions to which they devoted themselves, there was no shortage of vocations. Between 1841 and 1845, twenty-five took the veil, and eighteen of these persevered. On September 15, 1844, Mother Mary of the Seven Dolors and three companions professed the three religious vows at a Mass celebrated by Father Moreau. Since the bishop did not want to recognize them as religious but only as a confraternity of "pious girls," there was no additional ceremony. It was not until 1867, after Bishop Bouvier's death, that their constitutions were approved, and then with important changes in their functions and in their legal relationship to the other branches of Holy Cross.

With the establishment of the sisters, the Congregation had assumed its definitive form. As has been seen, it developed experimentally and pragmatically in relation to means and opportunities at the founder's disposal. It was, nevertheless, the result of a thoroughly thought-out plan, a fact established by Father Moreau's circular letter of September 1, 1841.

This letter stresses the ideal of a life of perfection based on obedience, discipline, punctuality, community spirit, zeal for the interior life, edification, and devotion to work. The priesthood occupied the central position in the plan, the brothers being associated with the priests to perform services for them and also to teach in their own elementary schools, while the sisters look after the house and the infirmaries. All of these concepts are developed in scriptural words and references. Father Moreau's years as a professor of scripture represented a major formative influence, giving him a familiarity with the content of both old and new testaments. His letters abound with quotations, while the influence on his thinking and attitudes goes much deeper.

As the basic spirit and organization assumed clear shape, the rate of growth and expansion increased, each day bringing its consolations and problems. The fame of the new foundation spread rapidly, and very soon Father Moreau was receiving appeals for help from many parts of France and even from across the sea.

One of his purposes was the giving of missions, and in his intention this activity was bounded only by the need. His early dream as a seminarian had been to dedicate his life to the foreign missions; he now saw the possibility of realizing that dream a hundredfold. And in fact, in a short time he would be able from the superabundance of his zeal to establish foundations in many countries and many continents. The story of these developments will be told in detail later, but for the moment it is necessary to return to the problems of growth as they affected the mother house and the various activities at Sainte-Croix, which constituted the material and moral basis of the entire work.

Political instability and social tension marked the life of France during the entire nineteenth century. Resistance to the development of new Catholic social forms was sometimes acute, sometimes less extreme. But it was always present, and people like Father Moreau had to struggle constantly to exercise the rights that post-Revolution France promised all citizens.

A basic problem was that a religious congregation, having no legal personality, could own no property. Its members, however, could form a civil society by pooling their property, work, and income. The Holy Cross Society had an equal number of brothers and priests, with Father Moreau as director. Later, he added laymen, both to reduce the risk of a charge that the civil society was an evasion of the law against religious congregations and to stimulate outside interest in Holy Cross.

Equally pressing was the need to secure teaching rights for Holy Cross schools, a point on which Father Moreau was inflexible. He considered the state's claims to monopoly in certain levels of education as absolutely unjust. It was a subject on which wide divergence of opinion existed both among Church groups and their opponents. Efforts were frequently made to liberalize the laws, but they were always sidetracked by political maneuvering and never brought to a vote. Indeed, it was not until 1841 that the hierarchy got together to oppose the state's denial of academic freedom in the name of political freedom.

To complicate things further, some still hankered after the old regime and rejected any solution of Church-State relations other than restoration of the society that had died with the Revolution.

Old wounds were reopened as the political pendulum swung now to the right, now to the left. The Revolution of 1830 provoked a sharp outbreak of persecution, which in turn produced an extraordinary Catholic upsurge. Again in 1848, the far more radical outburst made many anticipate a repetition of the entire cycle of the first explosion of 1789, with its bloodbaths and reigns of terror.

Father Moreau's attitude toward the secular power showed his common sense and his understanding of the dynamics of the situation. He was quick to isolate the false philosophic principle of the "liberals" as constituting the real issue for the Church. Time and again he recorded his view that education must incorporate a genuine philosophy and that the wrong attitudes formed in the state institutions encouraged the young to become skeptics or pantheists.

Nor was the state content with reaching only those in its own educational institutions. On the contrary, it sought to control the administration of all programs and indeed to exercise a complete monopoly. Nonstate institutions were treated as rivals of the state and engaged in an inherently antisocial activity, to be tolerated only until the state's services were sufficiently organized and financed to absorb their facilities.

The state university was the instrument used to implement this program. Its authority extended not only to publicly financed schools but also to such private schools as were tolerated. Different school levels were carefully distinguished. Apart from strictly primary schools, there were boarding schools where Latin grammar was taught along with primary subjects; institutes, corresponding roughly to junior high schools, with two years of humanities; and colleges, similar to high schools and junior colleges in the American system, with a full course in humanities and philosophy.

Father Moreau's goal was college status, but that had to wait. He did, however, win recognition as an "institute" in 1838, and he set out immediately to demonstrate the value of academic freedom within a religious framework. Although the university authorities treated him as an enemy, he tried to show by positive acts that he wanted cooperation and that his ultimate aim was an affiliation to enable his students to take the state examinations on the basis of work done in his classrooms.

As a first step, he assembled top-level teachers and encouraged them both to improve their qualifications and to prepare and publish textbooks. He then promoted a distinguishing atmosphere of true liberalism, far more in step with the times than the pseudo-liberalism of his opponents. For the traditional military apartness, with the professors constituting a class aloof from and emotionally uninvolved with the students, like army officers toward enlisted men, he substituted a friendly relationship based on the concept of the Holy Family. He did not outlaw punishment, but he rejected theories which glorified it as an integral element in training and reserved it for situations where all else had failed. This, of course, every educator claims to do, so a specific instance may help to clarify Father Moreau's position.

The Revolution of 1848 produced an unparalleled emotional reaction all across Europe. Barricades rose in the streets of capital after capital as a paradoxical symbol of liberty and often as an excuse for license. The fever caught Holy Cross. Several members abandoned their vocation, and, while the triumphant anticlericals moved to destroy this nest of "crypto-Jesuits," the students got into the act, forming leadership committees, starting military exercises, and formulating demands for a regime more to their liking.

Father Moreau had an amazing ability for placing day-to-day events in an historical perspective. He insisted now, as always, that the Church had no business in politics and could adjust itself to any political regime that would recognize its right to operate in its own sphere. This attitude, of course, pleased the extremists on neither side. He was publicly attacked by an atheistic mayor for his "political indifferentism," and he also caused no little unhappiness to his more intransigent colleagues by declaring that in some ways a republican government created a better climate for the development of the Church than did a monarchy. Similarly, he voiced no objection to the students' high spirits when the Second Republic was declared, allowing them to join with their band in civic celebrations.

He had to draw the line, however, when they challenged the school administration. And when he did, the reaction was an open revolt. The students seized part of the buildings and declared their own Barricade Day. The tension was acute, but Father Moreau kept perfectly cool. He had tremendous persuasive ability, which he now used to such effect that before long they came out one by one and assembled in a study hall. There he subjected them to a verbal blistering, rejected their demands, and promised expulsion for the slightest new violation. And with that he dismissed them, imposing absolutely no punishment, not even on the ringleaders.

The formula worked. That was the end of revolution inside Sainte-Croix. And the same moderate approach succeeded with the enemies outside. When the danger developed that the extremist elements would forcibly close Sainte-Croix, the workers in the neighborhood organized parties to maintain a constant guard. A reaction to all the violence soon set in, and, when more moderate elements emerged in government, Father Moreau seized the opportunity to win for himself the rights proclaimed for all by the Revolution. Despite outraged protests from the local anticlerical press, Sainte-Croix was given full teaching privileges in January 1849. The favor was well earned, for the school was already the most important Catholic institution of secondary education in the west of France. But it was also a tremendous vindication of the stand he had adopted.

His delight at being able to teach philosophy was unbounded, for he had felt that his work was less than half done so long as the students had to go from Sainte-Croix to the university to be indoctrinated with a materialistic outlook on life. He had a modern and practical approach to the content of education, always insisting that education was intended to prepare for living and that the vast majority of the students were going to live in the world. He consequently opposed the common view that a school for training community leaders should follow a regime similar to that of a seminary, and he added to the traditional subjects courses in the fine arts, physical education, and dancing. Such an attitude, today commonplace, was then revolutionary.

He equally insisted on the integration of religion into education. A major contribution in this area was a textbook he prepared, a symposium of Christian thought through the ages, drawing heavily on Scripture and the Church Fathers. This book was extremely successful and went through many editions and revisions. Another valuable help toward creating a philosophy of education for all Holy Cross teachers was a *Teacher's Guide*, in which he set out his theoretical and practical approach. Among devotional exercises, he particularly recommended frequent Holy Communion, in which he was again far ahead of contemporary opinion.

Many details of the early years are recorded in an annual volume first published in 1840 called *Etrennes spirituelles*. It had many of the characteristics of an almanac but with each story or piece of advice interpreted in spiritual terms. Father Moreau wrote much of the text, developing his characteristic thoughts. His purpose was to influence people to intensify their spiritual life and at the same time to spread information about Holy Cross and obtain both the backing of public opinion and financial aid. The annual went to all members of the Association of the Good Shepherd and of the Association of St. Joseph. A typical article analyzes the development of the notion of charity in the synagogue and the church, proclaiming this to be the true revolution marking human progress.

Another function of the annual was to answer calumnies, whether against the Church or against Holy Cross. Accordingly, one finds in it echoes of the virulent propaganda conducted against the Jesuits, indulgences, miracles, and devotion to our Lady in the anticlerical press of the day.

The expansion of Holy Cross itself outraged the enemies of religion, and the importance of Father Moreau's work is reflected in the attention they gave him not only locally but in their Paris mouthpieces. It was his practice to treat every calumny seriously and to set out the facts in scrupulous detail, especially if accused of obtaining money by unfair pressure or false pretenses. Such charges were frequent, for a constant refrain of the anticlericals was that the clergy's first concern was to make a good living.

Father Moreau had an admirable, almost ingenuous, belief in the inevitable triumph of truth and justice, and he sought to demonstrate by daily test what is usually applicable only to the secular sweep of history and to the patience of the divine plan. Thus he constantly defended the brothers in their scattered schools (which numbered about fifty at this period) against petty local opposition, taking his case to the education minister in Paris when he felt that subordinates were being unfair.

Usually the points at issue involved tricky political maneuvering in which the brothers were pawns in a vaster game, a procedure at which the French have always been adept. A local school board or a village council wanted the brothers but the district board sat on the application. A brother's salary was withheld on a claim of unsatisfactory performance, yet when the outraged brother hung out a shingle as a freelance teacher, he soon attracted a hundred pupils and had to enlist a helper.

Father Moreau was right in recognizing the injustice, and one can sympathize with his efforts to correct it. Yet, the facts of small-time politics arc always the same. When the red herrings have been dragged across the trails and the skeletons brought forth from the closets, nobody can recall what the row was about in the first place. And when the smoke clears, what remain are damaged reputations and hurt egos, and a sense of grievance all round. Father Moreau's adversaries were clever. They even managed at times to jockey local pastors into their camp. One pastor joined a school committee in signing a document objecting to establishment of a school on the stated ground that the brothers were bound by obedience and might get orders from their religious superiors in conflict with the civil law. Such was the power of Gallicanism.

Judgment on Father Moreau's methods will vary with the viewpoint of the observer. Some favor the wisdom of the serpent, others the simplicity of the dove. All can agree, however, that the man who in every circumstance appeals to the jury of public opinion to judge the justice of his cause risks disillusionment for many. And such is in large part the story of Father Moreau's life. But was he wrong to do this? In the perspective of history and the brilliance of his works that still live, who will say that he was?

In May 1840, a few months before the first issue of the annual, Father Moreau announced that he was going to build at Sainte-Croix a big conventual church, in gratitude (as he said) to our Lady and the Holy Cross for all favors granted his spiritual family, and also to help implement plans for a retreat house.

Ground was broken the same year, and in 1842 three bells were installed. These were made the occasion for one of the spectacular ceremonies characteristic of his missionary technique. They were presented as symbolic representations of the priests, the brothers, and the sisters the first dedicated to the Sacred Heart of Jesus, the second to the Holy Heart of Mary, and the third to St. Joseph.

Father Moreau regarded that church to be one of his most significant undertakings and worked feverishly to raise funds for it. He considered it a highlight of his life when Bishop Bouvier came to bless the cornerstone and encourage the project. He saw this solid monument dominating the district as a symbol of the permanence of his work, just as it was a symbol and a taunt for the enemies of that work. He persevered with it and completed it. The enemies withdrew in baffled fury. But they did not give up. Their turn would come.

The church also symbolized a personal decision for Father Moreau. He was committing himself irrevocably to Holy Cross. Up until now, this activity might have been only another step toward an ulterior goal. It had made itself for him. He had been drawn into it by the development of events in much the same way as he had become a professor and director of the Good Shepherd sisters.

But the church was a decisive act of involvement. It committed him physically in terms of long hours of manual work alongside the masons and carpenters, and of still more time and effort in raising funds to pay the workmen. It committed him emotionally, for he saw this building as the exterior expression of his own personal dedication and that of his companions to God.

Many questioned the wisdom of so elaborate a monument at a time when the current needs of his growing family were acute. To him the question was meaningless. None of its needs was more immediate than a family home, and a church is the home of a spiritual family. He worked at it with feverish haste, as if he feared the devil might at any moment find a way to stop him.

By 1845, one could see a spacious nave in neo-Gothic style. The first religious service for the community was celebrated on the Feast of the Assumption, 1846. On the following Palm Sunday, the church was opened for the general faithful. Father Moreau could rejoice as he admired the visible image of the invisible and spiritual edifice of Holy Cross.

CHAPTER EIGHT

First Foundations in America

As important as a home was for the personality of the Congregation of Holy Cross, this required both ecclesiastical and civil recognition. Father Moreau was very clear in his own mind as to the solution of the problem. In the long run, the kind of organization he was building called for a status which would enable it to function freely everywhere. This meant, among other things, that ecclesiastical approval had to be from Rome.

Father Moreau knew that the physical expansion of his institute outside the diocese of Le Mans would count as a powerful argument with Rome for its approval as a pontifical association. Such expansion was also most welcome to him personally in so far as it meant sending missionaries to spread the Gospel overseas. Accordingly, during the same years in which he was building the mother church at Sainte-Croix, he was working day and night to achieve this wider aim.

Father Mollevaut had a hand in the first requests for missionaries. He was probably responsible for bringing Holy Cross to the attention of Bishop Dupuch of Algiers, who in 1839 requested three brothers immediately and several others later. And he was

113

definitely the intermediary on behalf of Bishop-Elect de la Hailandière of Vincennes, Indiana, who appealed for priests and brothers in that same year, and for Bishop Bourget of Montreal, who visited Sainte-Croix two years later.

At first Father Moreau hesitated. He could see clearly the reasons in favor of a mission foundation, yet his primary duty was to protect his infant society, and he feared the additional strain on its meager resources. Father Mollevaut encouraged him to push ahead. He agreed that there were risks involved in excessive dissipation of effort, but he urged that the extreme need left no choice but to try.

Algeria seemed the likely place for a beginning. The fact that French was to be the school language would simplify matters; what's more, a contribution in Algeria would provide leverage with the French education authorities in Paris. Ten years earlier France had annexed Algeria, and its rule was not yet solidly established even in the north. Living conditions were incredibly backward and the economy most rudimentary. Indeed it was only twenty or twenty-five years since the European powers, with the help of the United States, had succeeded in curbing the country's main activity and source of income for over a century—large-scale piracy and holding of captives for ransom.

The first Holy Cross contingent sailed from Marseille for Algiers in May 1840, with Father Drouelle as superior and Father Boucher to take charge of the minor seminary. Their companions were two professed brothers, André and Alphonse, and two brothers who were still novices, Ignace and Victor. The obstacles inherent in the experiment were compounded by the vagaries of French policy. The administrators were not only steeped in French anticlericalism; they were also most anxious to avoid friction with the Moslem Algerians by seeming to promote any form of Christianity. Consequently, while they welcomed desperately needed teachers they wanted them to restrict their activities to a degree incompatible with the sense of mission of the new apostles of Holy Cross.

The priests and brothers started out on a variety of good works, schools, a minor seminary, and parishes, but official resistance and the lack of funds forced Father Moreau to recall all of them in June 1842. He refused, nevertheless, to regard this setback as final, and the next year he got government approval for the return of the brothers as teachers. Six brothers went back, but the authorities still refused to authorize a priest even as superior.

In the arid desert, a plant takes much tending and gives slight return. The swirling sand-laden sirocco quickly blots out the traces of one's toil. So it was with Holy Cross. Though the brothers labored and suffered in Algeria until 1873, the only monument to their efforts is the writing in the Book of Life. No subsequent effort was made to re-establish in Algeria, but today Holy Cross is working elsewhere in Africa, in Ghana, Kenya, Tanzania, and Uganda.

Nor did Father Moreau obtain another benefit he had hoped to win by sending brothers to Algeria. He had counted on the Education Minister of the French Government to back an application to have the brothers civilly recognized as a religious congregation. The Minister was happy to use the brothers, but, when the application was made, he sidestepped an answer. The bishops of France, he suggested, might not want a new institute competing with the Christian Brothers.

Father Moreau's reaction was typical. He asked the bishops, every one of them, and fifty-seven replied favorably, for the fame of Holy Cross had spread across the country. Several asked how soon they could get brothers to open schools in their dioceses, and all expressed the hope that they would have them one day. The outcome of the episcopal referendum was gratifying, but it did not budge officialdom. Father Moreau had to be content with an approval from the colonial ministry for work in Algeria.

By this time, however, another development had taken place to reduce the importance of Algeria in Father Moreau's plans both as a mission field for Holy Cross and as a lever to secure the approval so essential to the normal functioning of his society. Seed planted on the other side of the Atlantic had fallen on more fertile ground. Each year it became more obvious that in this mission Holy Cross would soon be helping significantly in the progress of the Church.

Even before this time, the French contribution to the Church in the United States was substantial, especially in the Midwest. When the second Provincial Council of Baltimore met in 1833, three of the country's ten bishops and seventy of its 380 priests were French. This council asked Rome to create the diocese of Vincennes, embracing the entire state of Indiana and part of Illinois. Simon William Bruté de Rémur, named bishop the following year, was a Frenchman who had earlier taught at Rennes, where he knew the Lamennais brothers. After his installation in 1834, he went to Europe for two years to recruit priests, as American bishops often did in those days.

One of sixteen volunteers he succeeded in obtaining was a Father de la Hailandière, whom he sent again to Europe in 1839 on a further recruiting mission. While there, he was appointed coadjutor with right of succession, and, a few weeks later, Bishop Bruté de Rémur died. The news of his bishop's death and his own consequent elevation reached Father de la Hailandiére at St. Sulpice, Paris. Only with the strong encouragement of Father Mollevaut, and his promise to help in recruiting clergy for the diocese, did he reluctantly accept.

It was no easy assignment. Indiana, with an area of thirty-six thousand square miles and a population of almost seven hundred thousand had few Catholics and only twenty priests. If the Catholic population was increasing with the influx of immigrants of various nationalities, so was the bigotry and the opposition to the "papist invasion."

On Father Mollevaut's recommendation, Bishop de la Hailandière wrote to Sainte-Croix and later paid a visit there. The story he told aroused Father Moreau's apostolic enthusiasm but did little to quiet his doubts as an administrator. The bishop was very vague about finances. He first suggested that Father Moreau decide whether the new house be provided by the bishop and remain his property or be financed by and remain dependent on Holy Cross. Soon it emerged that the bishop didn't have money even to pay passages. All he could offer was a farm in Indiana, on which the missionaries could build.

Financial considerations, however, never turned Father Moreau aside from a worthwhile objective. The Associates of St. Joseph got permission to run a lottery, and on its proceeds the first members of Holy Cross left for America in August 1841.

Bishop de la Hailandière had requested three or four brother teachers and a priest to be their superior and director. With a fine sense of the needs of the new world, Father Moreau sent not only three teachers, Brothers Vincent, Anselm, and Gatian, but a brother tailor, a brother carpenter, and a brother farmer, named respectively Joachim, Francis Xavier, and Lawrence. All of them would find plenty of opportunity to practice their trades in the wilderness.

With the six brothers went as superior a priest destined to prove next in importance to Father Moreau himself in developing and shaping Holy Cross. He was Edward Sorin de la Gaulterie, fifteen years younger than the founder and a member of Holy Cross for only two. He was one of the first group of Auxiliary Priests to profess religious vows on August 15, 1840.

Sailing from Le Havre on August 8, they reached New York thirty-six days later. Transcontinental railroads were still a dream of the future, so the next stage was a steamboat on the Hudson, through the canal to Buffalo, New York, on a horse-drawn barge, across Lake Erie to Toledo, Ohio, again by canal to the town of Napoleon in Indiana, and the final sixty miles by forest trails to Vincennes.

Father Sorin was a typical tourist. Along the route he counted the bridges and locks. He was in constant admiration of the grandeur of the scenery, of which he wrote that "nature has never been painted with bolder strokes." A stop at Lockport enabled him and a companion to go by rail to see Niagara Falls, which he contemplated "on his knees"; and, having made a cross out of two elm branches, he planted it in the earth, like a sixteenth-century conquistador.

The forced march through the forest was rugged, but the enthusiasm and fervor never failed. On Sunday morning, October 10, they walked fasting three and a half hours across the sandy country to reach Vincennes for Mass at nine.

The bishop's early indecision continued. A community was started and some money raised. Four postulants joined the newcomers, and several others talked of entering. But the central problem of canonical status remained unsolved. The bishop wanted the control in his own hands but lacked funds to underwrite the community, and Father Moreau insisted that, if he had to cover the cost of the mission, there could be no question about his continuing jurisdiction over it.

Notwithstanding the basic uncertainty, Father Sorin embarked on various projects. In glowing terms he reported the extent of the need and of the opportunity, and Father Moreau agreed not only to send more brothers but to underwrite all costs of the American mission and keep it independent of the diocese. The bishop was delighted with the extra help and the money, but he still wanted to wiggle out of his part of the bargain. He even wrote to Father Moreau that Father Sorin would prefer the mother house to bow out of the picture and let him deal directly with the bishop. In the light of the subsequent events, the possibility of Father Sorin's having said as much cannot be excluded. However, there is no independent confirmation, and Father Moreau retained complete faith in him and continued to help.

One may recall the similar clash of jurisdiction in the Good Shepherd case. One reason for it was that the canonical rules were less precise than now. Another was that few knew their canon law. And, finally, delegates often had inadequate training in their duties as religious. In Vincennes, a new dimension was added, that of time and distance. It was four thousand miles from

France. It took three or more months to get an answer to an urgent question.

The easy way out was a formula to please everyone, rather than a showdown on what seemed a somewhat speculative issue. The formula was found when the bishop visited Sainte-Croix in February 1845. He signed an agreement recognizing the dependence of the foundations in his diocese on Holy Cross, "while still regarding the worthy bishop as their local superior." Would more precise wording have avoided the subsequent clashes? Certainly the vagueness made it harder to resolve them when they came.

The bishop of Montreal, as already noted, had come to Sainte-Croix in 1841 in search of missionaries. He, however, had to wait six years before his request was fulfilled. It was not until May 1847 that the first contingent consisting of two priests, eight brothers, and four sisters arrived in Montreal to establish foundations at St. Laurent and Terrebonne.

Adjustment to Canada was easier than to the United States. No new language had to be learned, and the tempo of life and social attitudes were much closer to those of France. The problems, too, were largely those to which they were accustomed, and most of all poverty, even more pressing than it had been at home. But, as in France, they managed to survive and to win the same kind of reputation for zeal and devotion. Progress would be less spectacular than in the United States, but the tensions of growth would be less acute. Canada would never give Father Moreau serious worries. He could always rely on it to share its meager resources.

With the progress in the missions overseas, Father Moreau naturally thought of enlisting the aid of the bishops there in order to secure the coveted approval of the Holy See. As early as September 1843, he had consulted the papal nuncio in Paris as to the best way to approach Rome. The nuncio had replied in a gracious but noncommittal letter. He recommended that a report detailing the work of the Congregation be sent direct to Rome, accompanied by "a recommendation from His Lordship, the Bishop," since "it is always the practice of the Holy See to take no action in such cases without first hearing what the bishops have to say."

Unfortunately, as Father Moreau well knew, the bishop of Le Mans would have nothing good to say. As far as the brothers were concerned, he had approved them, though in a form falling far short of what Father Moreau envisaged. An agreement had also been reached in principle as regards the priests. But he would have no part of the "pious girls" whom Father Moreau wanted to enjoy the full status of religious and to integrate into the structure of the future Congregation of Holy Cross.

In this impasse, he wrote to Father Sorin suggesting that he might establish the Marianite Sisters canonically in the United States and get a bishop there to approve them with Father Sorin as superior. Almost by return mail he was informed that not only one but two bishops were willing to accept the role. What had happened was that the bishop of Detroit was urging Father Sorin to move his headquarters from Vincennes, and the bishop of Vincennes for his part did not want to lose him. Either was ready to assume responsibility for the move. "I have no hesitation," wrote the bishop of Detroit, "in giving my assent and my episcopal approbation to the founding of the community in my diocese, and to giving it diocesan status as soon as the Sisters are established there."

Encouraged by this progress, Father Moreau decided to try once more for Rome's approval. He submitted a memorandum to the nuncio describing the work in the schools in France and in the foundations abroad, and he appended a list of the favorable responses received from more than sixty bishops. This was followed shortly by a copy of an agreement signed by the bishop of Vincennes, who would not be outdone by his colleague of Detroit and had accordingly approved for his diocese "the priests, brothers and sisters of Holy Cross" and authorized them "to follow their constitutions."

The one essential bishop was, nevertheless, still absent from the list. Rome was extremely sympathetic to Father Moreau and anxious to show its favor. In August 1846, the Congregation of Propaganda accorded him the title of Apostolic Missionary. The nuncio had recommended the request as coming from "a most deserving and very holy priest" of Le Mans, already known to the Sacred Congregation. The title granted him personally a certain degree of exemption from his bishop, since he received his faculties directly from the pope. But the privilege was exclusively for himself. It did nothing concrete for the society of which he was superior, though it was proof of interest on the part of the Holy See.

And Rome would not go over the bishop's head. On receiving the memorandum from the nuncio describing the progress of Holy Cross, the Congregation of Bishops and Regulars asked Bishop Bouvier for his opinion. His answer was a resounding no. "I do not feel that the constitutions of this society should be approved until it has proved itself by a longer and more successful period of trial."

As was inevitable, Rome accepted the bishop's viewpoint. In September 1846, the Sacred Congregation wrote to him to assure him that no approbation would be forthcoming.

Father Moreau knew of the Sacred Congregation's enquiry addressed to Bishop Bouvier but nothing about the subsequent developments. After a delay of several months, he decided to try once more, this time with a petition to the Holy Father himself. It was signed by the thirteen members who, with their superior, constituted the chapter of priests at Sainte-Croix, and it described the activities of the priests and brothers. It listed the priests as numbering twenty-two, with twelve novices; and the brothers as 182, in charge of fifty-nine schools in various dioceses of France, in Algeria, in Vincennes and Detroit in the United States, and in Montreal, Canada. The sisters were also mentioned. They numbered thirty-five, of whom twelve were professed. They were in charge of four schools in America.

The only effect this communication had in Rome was to irritate officials who had made a decision and had no desire to reconsider. Word of it apparently also got to Bishop Bouvier and caused a further deterioration of relations with him. He protested to the nuncio in Paris that Father Moreau was going over his head and asking other bishops to bring pressure to bear on the Holy See. The nuncio answered curtly, ending the particular incident, but not the bishop's annoyance. Another grievance was caused when Father Moreau had the Constitutions printed and distributed to the members of the Congregation without submitting them for the bishop's approval. The latter actually went to the length of starting a competing diocesan organization of missionary priests, and two professed priests left Holy Cross to join the group. It was a new blow to the prestige of the Congregation.

When to this was added a reply from Rome rejecting the latest approaches made on his behalf, Father Moreau decided that he was personally at fault. With characteristic humility he threw himself on the mercy of the bishop, accepting the blame for whatever he had done against the bishop's wishes and offering to resign in order to permit a new start at Holy Cross. The bishop seemed impressed. After a series of discussions, he refused the resignation, and went so far as to preside at the opening of the students' retreat in October 1849.

Not only the bishop but also the members of Holy Cross gave a vote of confidence to the founder this same year. He had been elected to the office of superior general in 1843 and again in 1846. The Constitutions provided that election for a third term was automatically election for life.

When the general chapter of 1849 took up the question, Father Moreau begged them to pick someone else. He said he would gladly assist his successor with his advice, and that he would carry out any assignments given him, whether at Sainte-Croix, in the preaching apostolate, or on the foreign missions. His disappearance from the scene, he urged, might help silence such complaints as had been raised against his administration.

The chapter, however, refused to countenance the request. There was general agreement that only a continuance of his prudent and firm government could guarantee the completion of the work well begun. He accepted the decision with his usual humility and immediately returned with renewed zeal to the task of developing the moral and religious personality of the Congregation.

Always intent on approval, he visited Rome the following year and had several audiences with Pope Pius IX, on whom he made a most favorable impression, and by whom he was given striking marks of regard.

The visit to Rome resulted from a request to establish an orphanage. During the previous years of revolution and disturbance, Rome had suffered tremendously, especially when Garibaldi's armies occupied the city and forced the Pope to flee. A French expedition soon ejected the invaders, but the effects of the disturbances would take long to eliminate.

Pius IX was concerned equally about the immediate needs of the victims and about the long-term requirements of the city for which he was responsible both as bishop and civil ruler. He was delighted when informed that Holy Cross was prepared to take over a foundation for boys recently started by a Russian princess.

Santa Prisca Orphanage was in extreme disorder, and Father Moreau soon saw that he could count neither on the staff nor on the ecclesiastical superior. Nevertheless, he threw himself into the task and, with the help and example of four of his own brothers, slowly began to impose discipline, to the amazement and delight of Monsignor Xavier de Mérode, secret chamberlain of the Pope, who just then was entrusted by the Holy Father with supervision of the work for abandoned children. His friendship with Father Moreau was to be of considerable significance to Holy Cross.

Msgr. de Mérode belonged to the Belgian aristocracy on his father's side and to that of France on his mother's. He was a brother-in-law of Montalembert, the French journalist and politician, cofounder with Lamennais of the journal *L'Avenir* in which they upheld the interests of the Catholic Church and the clergy. Montalembert advised an army career, as did the nuncio in Brussels who later became Leo XII but after graduation from military college and service in Africa, de Mérode entered a seminary and became a priest. This did not, however, end his military associations, for Pius IX made him Minister of the Army when he recruited volunteers to defend the Papal States. He was an unusual man, standing out as the incarnation of devotion to the Holy See, and Father Moreau was completely captivated by him. But, as would gradually emerge, the man was also extremely inconsistent, and this would cause great trouble in the course of the development of the Holy Cross foundations in Rome.

Father Moreau's first audience with Pius IX is described at length in a letter written the same day, which does equal credit to the writer and his subject. This was the highlight of a full life. Encouraged by the Pope, who had been briefed in advance, Father Moreau poured out his emotions. He was a Roman at heart, he affirmed, attached to the Holy See by his innermost sentiments and by his theological training. He had at Sainte-Croix three societies in one, priests who taught and preached missions, brothers who taught primary and trade schools, and sisters who cared for the poor and engaged in other humble activities.

And he had nothing when he began his congregation? Pius asked. Nothing, he replied, yet he had spent more than two million francs on Holy Cross and on the Good Shepherd convent at Le Mans.

The mention of money reminded him that friends had given him two hundred francs for the Pope. This gesture produced a corresponding response on the Pope's part. He called for his chamberlain and handed Father Moreau five thousand francs for the Holy Cross orphanage in Rome.

Father Moreau then requested various spiritual favors for Holy Cross, and Pius, granted them over his own signature. This in turn led to further discussions and an examination of the plans of the mother house, Father Moreau informing His Holiness proudly that a steam pump carried water to all parts of the property. It sounded fine, said Pius when he had heard the whole story, "but all that is communism!"

Father Moreau was perfectly at ease. "Holy Father, this is what I told the workingmen at Le Mans who wanted to loot us in 1848. When I showed them Sainte-Croix in detail, they set up guards all around to protect us."

From the moment of his arrival, Father Moreau was thrilled by Rome. He was overawed, as he wrote, at the sight of the countless basilicas, ancient temples, triumphal arches, obelisks, columns, and statues. For one so attached to Rome and the papacy, it was natural that St. Peter's should have a special meaning. It was the first place he chose to visit. He returned there some days later on the feast of its dedication, and that same evening he wrote his community at Sainte-Croix an account of the experience. He had seen the tomb of the Prince of the Apostles glistening with lights, the altar where only the Pope may officiate, the colossal statue on the right side of the main nave, and the chair of St. Peter. He had venerated the relics exposed that day: Veronica's veil, the lance of Longinus, a portion of the True Cross, the head of St. Andrew.

Then, all of a sudden, he had perceived the "angelic figure of Pius IX" presiding over the ceremony. Such was his emotion that, to the great scandal of the priests near him, he pushed aside the Swiss Guards, made his way through the cardinals, and threw himself on his knees before the Pope to kiss his feet. Pius IX smiled kindly. Father Moreau's heart was full to overflowing, and he went away overjoyed.

"I was beside myself," he wrote in his account of this memorable day.

> I wept and thanked the Providence which had at last brought me to the Eternal City. May you, my friends, have this grace some day! Your faith would

be re-enkindled, for here—so to speak—one can put one's fingers on the facts of Christianity and the deeds of the Apostles. May St. Peter, whose image and precious remains I have just venerated, obtain for you the grace to love Jesus Christ as he did.

Father Moreau was received in special audience many times by the Pope, an indication both of the impact made by the new religious society and its founder, and of Pius's concern for his diocese and flock. On December 9, Father Moreau brought three of the brothers to a most informal audience, during which the Pope gave the orphanage a vineyard called Vigna Pia so that the boys could learn farming. Father Moreau triumphantly carried off the pen with which the Holy Father signed a document he submitted, to have pen and document framed and hung in his room at Sainte-Croix.

Pius IX followed Father Moreau's operating techniques with attention and obvious approval. Father Moreau had decided that conditions at Santa Prisca were unsatisfactory. There was space for only limited activities, and the official administration lacked drive. The Pope's vineyard had only the shell of a house on it, but there was room to expand, and, besides, they would be working under Msgr. de Mérode.

That was enough. Father Moreau moved in with a group of boys, and soon things were humming. He rounded up supplies to meet immediate needs and wrote to Sainte-Croix for more helpers and for tools. Everything was soon under control, and the Pope was delighted. One of his first acts after his coronation had been to buy this property for an agricultural orphanage, and the failure of those earlier plans had disappointed him.

The importance which Holy Cross quickly assumed in the Holy Father's plans is reflected in one of Father Moreau's letters. Msgr. de Mérode asked him to lunch, he wrote, and told him that the Pope had decided to remove his rabat. Rising from the table, the Monsignor led him through the palace halls to the papal apartments, where Pius advanced to meet him as he made the customary genuflections, grasped the rabat, and tossed it on the table.

This was a significant symbolic action, expressing the Holy Father's confidence in his visitor and his acceptance of the protestations Father Moreau had made at his first audience that he was a Roman at heart. The rabat, or rabato, a large collar of linen or lace, formed the distinguishing feature of French clerical dress. It had also become a symbol of Gallicanism and resistance to papal authority.

The gesture was intended—and was regarded by Father Moreau—as the Pope's adoption of him and his community. The next day, he was told, he would receive a little collar like the one worn by St. Vincent de Paul for himself and his religious, including the brothers. The Roman collar thus became part of the dress of the Congregation of Holy Cross.

The audience continued with new expressions of kindness. Pius blessed packages of medals, indulgenced a reliquary to contain a particle of the True Cross, granted indulgences for friends of Holy Cross and Father Moreau's family, and spoke words interpreted by Father Moreau as an anticipated approval of his Congregation: "I bless all your priests, all your brothers, all your sisters—the whole of your great family."

It was a moment of triumph, but still far from the goal of formal approval. Father Moreau's demonstration of the effective work and spirit of his society, and of his own organizing ability, was undoubtedly useful. And Pius IX's fulsome expressions of his esteem ensured a sympathetic consideration by the Roman officials. Nevertheless, so serious a matter required step-by-step progress through established procedures, and an essential step was a favorable report from the bishop in whose diocese the mother house was located. Father Moreau was so elated by his reception that he felt sure this obstacle could be surmounted. But he was wrong. The days lengthened to weeks and the weeks to months, and each day increased the pressures on Father Moreau to get back to Le Mans. Stay a little longer, his friends in Rome urged. We need you, came the cries from Holy Cross, ever more insistent, until he felt he could not ignore them. He left Rome in March 1851.

He was sure everything would be all right. A circular letter to his religious written two months later assured them that extraordinary news could be anticipated from Rome any day. But the news never came. Highly as Father Moreau and his work were esteemed in Rome, the conventions would continue to be observed. Bishop Bouvier's veto would not be overridden.

What did happen was that Rome found another way to show its appreciation of the work of Holy Cross and at the same time further test its resources and its spirit. In November, the Cardinal Prefect of the Congregation of Propaganda wrote to Father Moreau to ask if he would be willing to send missionaries to East Bengal, hinting very clearly at the same time that his response would weigh heavily with the Congregation of Propaganda on the question of approval.

There could be no doubt as to his answer. Quite apart from his absolute determination to do whatever might be required to win papal recognition, Father Moreau held no objective of Holy Cross higher than the foreign missions. "For several years now," he wrote to the Cardinal,

> not only myself but also all the priests and brothers of our Association, as well as the sisters, have felt ourselves impelled by the charity of our Lord Jesus Christ to undertake some apostolate to help the countless numbers of men who are still in the darkness of infidelity and the shadows of death.

While waiting for precise information about the location and scope of the mission, Father Moreau began to discuss which members of the Congregation would be best equipped for the task. As was his practice, he notified the diocesan chancery of the

names of priests who might, with the bishop's approval, be asked
to leave the diocese.

Bishop Bouvier had now reached a point where his opposition was almost automatic. He wrote scathingly to Rome that
Holy Cross could not possibly be of any use to the missions. They
could send men to Bengal only by taking them from the United
States, and the houses there needed all the subjects they had. In
addition, he accused Father Moreau of having exaggerated the
number of his subjects in a statement to Propaganda.

Father Drouelle, superior of the Holy Cross establishments
in Rome, relayed the charges to his superior general, and Father
Moreau replied point by point. He admitted that he planned
to send some English-speaking subjects from the United States
to Bengal, but he insisted that he had already sent others from
France to replace them. As for the membership of Holy Cross,
the count now showed forty-two more members than the four
hundred he had reported when he was in Rome.

Propaganda was convinced. In May 1852, it sent Bishop
Oliffe, Vicar Apostolic of East Bengal, to Sainte-Croix to make
the arrangements. He was in charge of a vast tropical territory
in which twenty million people lived in degradation and misery.
Most of them were Hindus or Muslims, and there were several
Protestant sects in the area that complicated things, even though
they had not made many converts. To add to the difficulty, a number of schismatic Catholic priests were in possession of the old
Catholic foundations, where they lived in relative comfort, manifesting no apostolic zeal and acting in complete independence
of the local hierarchy. Bishop Oliffe had only three or four priests
under his jurisdiction.

The first group set sail from London in November. It consisted of three priests, three brothers, and three sisters. Almost
immediately it began to encounter the trials which were to mark
this mission more than any other in the history of Holy Cross. A
violent storm smashed the mainmast and forced them to seek

shelter in a port in the south of England. One of the priests fell violently ill and was taken to a hospital, where he died.

The natural difficulties they encountered on arrival were extreme. The heat was almost insupportable for many months of the year. The missionaries had to learn three very difficult languages. They had to adjust themselves to a culture of which they had learned nothing beforehand. It was not long before catastrophes occurred to increase their suffering. The superior died of a fever in August 1855. That same month, a newly arrived priest and sister were drowned in an accident to a riverboat carrying them to their destination.

Nevertheless, the survivors continued to struggle along. In November of that same year, Bishop Oliffe was transferred to West Bengal, leaving the entire territory to be administered by Holy Cross. It had been the intention from the start that the next vicar-apostolic would be one of the missionaries, but nobody had anticipated that the change would come so soon and with so little preparation. Still, Father Moreau did not falter. He had been given an assignment, and he was determined to honor it. Father Pierre Dufal was proposed for the office of vicar-apostolic and approved by Rome, thus becoming the first Holy Cross bishop. His fifteen-year rule was to see amazing progress, including the healing of the schism, which had been a major handicap to the Church in Bengal.

During the same years, Holy Cross was expanding in yet another direction. Two years of negotiations culminated in 1856 in the inauguration of an agricultural orphanage—somewhat similar to the Vigna Pia Foundation in Rome—at Cracow, Poland. Although this experiment did not work out well and had to be abandoned in 1865, two other orphanages were opened in Poland, one at Poznan in 1851 and one at L'viv in 1868.

All of this progress was very gratifying to Father Moreau, yet it failed to secure the approval which he had hoped for his Congregation. Events had again proved him right and Bishop Bouvier wrong, but proving people wrong does not usually change their opinions. It certainly did not change the bishop's. Instead, yet another incident had occurred to harden him further in his opposition. He had been denounced as a heretic to Rome, and he suspected that Father Moreau had a part in the action.

What happened was that the tremendous success of his manual of theology had elevated him to the status of unofficial leader of the Gallican Party in France. But the opposition was growing stronger all the time, with the nuncio manifesting open sympathy for Dom Guéranger and its other leaders, until finally they succeeded in getting the Congregation of the Index to open a formal inquiry into the orthodoxy of the teaching in the Bouvier manual.

The bishop defended himself with his customary vigor, going in person to Rome. The nuncio urged formal condemnation, but more moderate views prevailed. Bishop Bouvier was allowed to revise his opinions in subsequent editions, thus escaping the embarrassment of a public retraction.

He accepted with laudable humility, but his emotional position remained unchanged. While recognizing the doctrinal correctness of the papal stand, he felt that Church administration was tending toward a dangerous centralization in Rome and that it was a bishop's duty to counter the trend. One can, accordingly, imagine his feelings on learning that Father Moreau and his associates had publicly switched allegiance by substituting the Roman collar for the rabat and that Father Moreau had issued instructions (as he did in 1851) that Holy Cross should use the Roman breviary exclusively for the divine office. Nor was he unaware of the rumors that Father Moreau and Dom Guéranger of Solesmes, both superiors of religious communities in his diocese, had led the movement to have his theology condemned.

Everyone in Rome, from the Holy Father down, sympathized with Father Moreau, and various pressures were applied. The bishop, however, was a seasoned tactician, always able to find a new excuse to replace one exposed by the other side. The Pope sided with him on the question of whether men and women religious should be combined under a single administration. There had been trouble enough of that kind with the Pipcus Congregation (also in France), the Pope said. This was a blow to Father Moreau, but he yielded when the Pope spoke, modifying his request so that it embraced only the priests and brothers. Bishop Bouvier soon found another pretext. They were too poor, he asserted, and saddled with immense debts. They lacked the material conditions required to guarantee permanence.

The Holy Cross foundations were indeed poor and had substantial debts, but, as Father Moreau insisted then and frequently, with detailed financial accounts to justify his position, they were solidly solvent. Assets considerably exceeded liabilities, and what they needed was the opportunity to utilize their human capital. He defended his Congregation with vigor and blamed himself when his arguments failed to achieve their aim. He begged the Pope to accept his resignation, for he was the one obstacle to the bishop's approval. Pius absolutely refused this solution, yet he would not override a distinguished French bishop who had just made his submission and undertaken to expurgate his works.

And so the deadlock continued. The strain on Father Moreau was tremendous. His dealings with the bishop were necessarily frequent. Sometimes a little of the old friendship revived. The bishop, for example, backed his request for civil recognition for Holy Cross, a benefit secured through the provincial prefect, whose wife was head of the Association of the Good Shepherd. However, when Father Moreau sought civil approval of Holy Cross as a charitable association, which would have given it additional legal rights, the bishop blocked the request.

The patience of Father Moreau and his companions was finally exhausted, and the general chapter told the bishop they would have to move the mother house. Father Moreau himself actually requested his *exeat*—a formal authorization to transfer to the jurisdiction of another bishop—an extreme step, which only the death of Bishop Bouvier prevented. Under his successor, the obstacles dissolved.

The effects were, however, unfortunately long-lasting. The union of the members of the Congregation was weakened by the drawn-out bickering, in which sides inevitably were taken. In Rome, too, the clash left its mark. People recalled it later when Father Moreau had to defend himself against serious charges. Where there was smoke, they said, there must be fire.

CHAPTER NINE

The Enigma of Father Sorin

Members of Holy Cross who knew Father Sorin as their superior general, a post he held from 1868 until his death in 1893, describe a gentle, affectionate, understanding father, a memory reinforced by photographs of the smiling, bearded patriarch. They recalled a priest who cast a magnetic spell over all who met him, revered by his colleagues, listened to with respect, and regarded as friend and equal by American bishops.

Is this the real Father Sorin? Real, yes, but certainly not complete. There were many Father Sorins, for here was a complex and volatile character, a man with a flair for drama and publicity, with a sense of the possible and the correlative drive to convert it into the actual, with a staggering self-assurance, and withal a deep spiritual commitment and a childlike devotion to the Mother of God.

"God alone can know what goes on in the soul which gives itself to him unreservedly and irrevocably." Father Sorin wrote this statement on the day he took vows in the Congregation of Holy Cross. It has a characteristic flamboyance, and it is often hard to say to what extent such recurring expressions reflect the man's true sentiments, and to what extent they are intended simply to impress. One need not doubt his basic sincerity, and yet it seems strange that he could quickly forget his protestations and behave as though his own will and viewpoint alone counted.

Edward Frederick Sorin's background was different from that of Basil Anthony Moreau. Born in 1814 to parents who belonged to the lesser country nobility, Sorin experienced neither the personal poverty nor the revolutionary upheavals which formed the other's youth. From a Catholic school, he went directly on to the seminary and ordination.

As a student he had a high sense of vocation, and mission aspirations were aroused in him by a visit to the seminary of a foreign missionary who, by a remarkable coincidence, came from the diocese of Vincennes, Indiana. On ordination he became an assistant pastor, but the desire for a more perfect life stayed with him, so that after one-year he joined Holy Cross. Under Father Moreau's direction, the generosity and energy of his character rapidly blossomed, and he was one of the four Auxiliary Priests who pronounced vows with Father Moreau on August 15, 1840.

Once the decision to send a band of missionaries to the United States was made, Father Sorin was the logical choice to lead it. There were several arguments against him. He was only twenty-six years old, three years a priest, and just out of the novitiate. But there was nobody else around of his caliber. He was energetic, spontaneous, sincere, open to the inspiration of great ideals, and sustained by an unfailing optimism. Father Moreau thought of him as his right hand. "What a sacrifice I have made," he exclaimed on wishing him godspeed.

From the first day, Father Sorin was at home in America. It took possession of him, and he of it. "Henceforth, I live only for my dear brethren in America," he had written even before setting sail. "America is my fatherland; it is the center of all my affections and the object of all my thoughts." The continent's immensity overwhelmed him, its youth, rapid growth, and flexibility. With prophetic insight he saw what all this meant for the Church, which had only to climb aboard, to adjust itself to the tempo and atmosphere of the new world as it had a thousand years earlier to that of the old.

His vocation was to help bring America and the Church together. This he understood, and it provided the driving force and motivation for all he did. Sometimes his sense of mission reached the exaggerated point of identification with the designs of providence. Then he became guilty of indiscreet, even objectively indefensible acts. There would be a series of recriminations and counter-recriminations between himself and his superiors in France. Tension would mount to the breaking point. He would withdraw from his objectively indefensible position, make elaborate promises to behave, and seemingly go right back to his old tricks.

Many factors must be assessed, however, before attempting to pass judgment. One was the vagueness of authority. Father Moreau conducted his affairs like a father with his children, not like a general with his troops. He did not spell out the details. When he loved and trusted one of his children to the extent to which he loved and trusted Father Sorin, he gave him wide discretion. When Father Sorin read into that discretion something the giver never anticipated and was reprimanded, he reacted like a child who feels his parent is unfair. This, I believe, is the only context in which the relations between the two over many years make sense.

Another psychological factor in Father Sorin's tendency to independence, it seems to me, was his success in establishing the first canonical foundation of the Marianites in America, while Father Moreau failed repeatedly to get episcopal recognition for them at home. It was understandable that he should think of himself as their founder in America (as Bishop Luers of Fort Wayne, Indiana, in fact described him) and that by his orders, his prohibitions, and his decisions he should seek to make himself the superior general in America, as Father Rézé complained to Father Moreau in 1852.

Slowness of communication and decision operated to strengthen this attitude. The Council at Le Mans might decree that no extraordinary expenditure should be made without its approval. But what happened in an emergency? The college at Notre Dame burned down. Did one wait three months for approval to rebuild? In three months public sympathy had evaporated, pupils had scattered to other schools. Either you did it right away or not at all.

This was an extreme case, but Father Sorin was rightly convinced that one had to adjust to the tempo of the United States, that the Church could win tremendous victories by moving fast. His vision was as vast as that of Father Moreau who saw in France the same need for extreme effort to prevent overwhelming defeat. The difference was that Father Sorin had given up hope for France. What was done for it was in his opinion wasted effort.

This judgment of Father Sorin on Europe was one of the basic causes of his drawn-out conflict with the mother house. "I praise God that I was not baptized under a French saint's name," he wrote. From the time of his first visit home to France in 1846, as he frequently said, he was convinced that there was no future there, and that "Divine Providence had sent us here and to Canada to prepare a home some day for the Congregation." Europe, he summed up, is "a domain now claimed by wicked angels, perverse passions, spirits of darkness, and embassies of the evil one.

These are not casual comments but formal judgments recorded in his circular letters as superior general. They help to reveal the mental processes behind some of Father Sorin's extraordinary maneuvers to get money from France or to avoid repayment. I don't pretend that they justify those maneuvers, for I think some of them unjustifiable, but they do make them more understandable. To invest the money in France was, in his view, to waste it, while to plow it into religious works in America was to build the Catholic Church of the future.

It must also be remembered that with today's hindsight we can say quite confidently that Father Sorin was right. If his judgment of Europe was extreme, his vision of America has been fully realized. And I think it can also be fairly asserted that Father Moreau was in full sympathy with his colleague's view of America. As the one both officially and personally responsible for all debts contracted by the mother house, he was understandably horrified by the presentation of unauthorized drafts or by failure to repay loans when he desperately needed funds. But if he sought to moderate the speed of movement, he never questioned its direction.

Father Charles Moreau, the founder's nephew and first biographer, inclines to blame his uncle for failing to curb Father Sorin, whom he disliked. "The good father, apart from his council," he wrote, "could refuse nothing which his conscience did not absolutely forbid." I think this is a misinterpretation of the situation. I think that, on the contrary, Father Moreau shared Father Sorin's own belief that none of their companions could make a success of the American experiment, and that the final effect of following his council's legalistic approach would be to destroy what good had been accomplished. It is noteworthy that even when Father Sorin was demoted and brought back to France after one of his more outrageous escapades (to be recounted shortly), Father Moreau chose to send him back to America and within a year to restore all his authority and discretion.

It has frequently been remarked that it would have made a great difference if Father Sorin had had the benefit of a deeper training in the religious life. No doubt this is true. Unlike his superior, who had the advantage of many years in St. Sulpice and as a professor at the seminary, all the time under the inspired guidance of Father Mollevaut, Father Sorin was sent off on his own as a very young man, with little foundation in the religious life beyond what he had acquired during his time in the novitiate.

But I think that his limited knowledge of theology was as important a factor as his inadequate understanding of obedience.

He would adopt a course of action which he instinctively knew to be correct but which he lacked the skill in casuistry to justify morally. Unable to defend his position when challenged, yet convinced he was right, he took refuge in evasions and ended up formally in the wrong. But the basic spirit of obedience did not die within him. Like Father Moreau himself, when faced with the supreme decision, Father Sorin sacrificed all he had built rather than maintain his own judgment against the voice of authority.

CHAPTER TEN

The Foundation at Notre Dame

Although for somewhat different reasons, Holy Cross had nearly as much trouble in reaching an understanding with the bishop of the diocese in which it made its first United States foundation as it had with the bishop of Le Mans.

Bishop de la Hailandière of Vincennes lacked both priests and money. To entice Father Moreau to send Father Sorin and his companions to Vincennes, he had made promises of support which he was totally unable to fulfill. But once he had these helpers, he was determined to hold on to them. He wanted them and all their activities to be under his entire control, even to the extent that they could not make foundations in other dioceses without his approval.

Such was certainly not the intention of either Father Moreau or Father Sorin, especially since they were paying the entire cost of the foundations. Father Sorin set out to develop the new establishments with all his customary energy, but he was quite unhappy because of the continued failure to come to an understanding with the bishop. Therefore, he accepted with enthusiasm when, in November 1842, the bishop offered him an Indian mission deep in the forests two hundred and more miles to the north. The change would not settle the theoretical dispute as to who had final control, but Father Sorin was confident that he could establish his practical independence at such a great distance, especially as the bishop guaranteed him "jurisdiction over everything you can visit."

It was the answer to his dream, the chance to carve out his portion of this unexploited land. He set off immediately, with no thought of waiting for approval from France. In this country things moved fast. You had to recognize your opportunity and seize it.

An eleven-day journey through snow against an icy wind failed to dampen his ardor. In high spirits he reached the mission, near the settlement of South Bend, Indiana, on November 22. The small mission house stood by a lake, now frozen over in a winter colder than any the Frenchman had ever experienced, which bore the appropriate and poetic name of Notre Dame du Lac, Our Lady of the Lake. This was Notre Dame. This would be Notre Dame.

In almost every letter written from Notre Dame, Father Sorin begged Father Moreau to send him sisters, and the first group of four left Le Mans in May 1843, together with three priests, Fathers Cointet, Marivault, and Gouësse. The sisters were all "Marys," according to custom: Mary of the Heart of Jesus, Mary of Calvary, Mary of Nazareth, and Mary of Bethlehem. From New York they followed the same route which Father Sorin had taken, up the Hudson and through the Great Lakes.

The sisters found plenty of work on arrival, for the clothing of all the community was in tatters. Nevertheless, they soon began to learn English and prepared to open two schools, one for the children of the settlers at South Bend and the other for those of the Indians at Pokagon. Three postulants joined the group almost immediately, and three more sisters arrived from France, so that the schools were inaugurated before the end of the year. The rapid start was an augury of what would follow. Before many years, Notre Dame would shelter more than half the entire group of Marianites.

Both Father Sorin and the bishop had understood from the outset that the principal feature of the new foundation would be a boarding school. When Father Sorin surveyed the scene, he agreed that everything favored the success of such a school. It could not fail to expand rapidly, he wrote Father Moreau, for it would be the one which "among all those of the United States" would be assured by its position of the best chances of success.

As for himself, however, he told his superior general in the same letter, that what he had seen had awakened in him an overpowering desire to consecrate his entire life to the Potawatomi Indians, and accordingly he wished to be relieved of his obligations as superior of Holy Cross in America. "Tomorrow, or rather today, I shall begin to study their language, and when your letter arrives I hope to be able to express my thanks in Indian."

But Father Sorin would never be tied down by what he said yesterday, and Father Moreau knew him too well to take his lyrical outburst seriously. The horizon of his vision quickly expanded. There was no reason why they could not have Indian missions and schools for the Indians as well as a high school for the settlers' children and a boarding school for boys coming from a distance. There was room at Notre Dame for everything.

Everything was soon to include a university. A member of the Indiana legislature who lived in nearby South Bend was so impressed by the rapid progress in the very first year that, though not himself a Catholic, he came to Father Sorin and offered to obtain a university charter for Notre Dame. Father Sorin thought it a wonderful idea. It would show them in France how things were done here. At Le Mans they had waited many years before their school achieved the status of an academy or high school. Here it was possible almost overnight to become a university.

Campus, faculty, student body, endowment, all these were lacking, but Notre Dame had its university, the third under Catholic auspices in the United States, after Georgetown and St. Louis.

That was enough for now; time would do the rest—time and the boundless energy and drive of Father Sorin.

Two years later, in 1845, the student enrollment had grown to thirty. The community itself had grown to thirty brothers, four sisters, two professed priests, two other priests, and a cleric in minor orders. Nine mission stations for the Indians organized within a radius of one hundred miles were visited regularly. Three hundred pupils were taught in five schools.

Money was being spent at a dizzying rate, for a residence for priests and brothers, for a convent for the sisters, for schools, for land clearance to grow food for the many mouths, for horses to transport the missionaries around their vast parish. Father Sorin took it all in stride. When he needed money, he borrowed. When he could not get a commercial loan, he went to a friend. When friends were exhausted, he issued a draft on Father Moreau. Sometimes he took the precaution to advise his superior to expect the draft. Sometimes he let the creditor arrive unannounced. It didn't seem too important. He was making an investment, sinking money wisely in the rich soil of a growing territory. This was the American way. Give it time, and it would justify itself.

Father Moreau, back at Sainte-Croix, was being driven to distraction. He was a man born and raised in poverty, knowing the value not only of a franc but of a sou. It was a constant struggle, aggravated by steady inflation, to meet his carefully calculated obligations. He was a stickler for accurate accounting and demanded advance approval of every extraordinary expenditure, both because he wanted to promote a spirit of religious poverty in his communities and because his resources were fully allocated and his credit constantly extended. He survived only by absolute restraint.

Their financial viewpoints certainly had nothing in common; it was only on a personal level that the two men might get along. Neither was the reaction of the general council at Sainte-Croix usually calculated to mend matters. Presentation of each unauthorized draft on Father Moreau led to a full-dress discussion of ways to clip Father Sorin's wings. The council would vote not to honor the unauthorized draft, as they had promised the previous time they would not, but Father Moreau would plead for one more chance. By a superhuman effort, he would raise the cash. There would be another lecture, another reminder of the obligation to incur no extraordinary expenditure without advance approval, another exposition of the mother house's desperate need to get back some of the previous short-term advances. When these had no effect, they would be reinforced by formal commands in virtue of the vow of obedience.

But the threats remained unfulfilled, and Father Sorin continued to play his hunches. For all his distress, Father Moreau continued basically to believe in him. He saw the good and constructive and generous aspects of his conduct. He knew that Father Sorin was right in his judgments as to what needed to be done to advance the interests of both Holy Cross and the Catholic Church in America.

Even the general council could not deny that fact. In a comment which exposed more than they suspected of the narrowness of their vision, they once summed up the situation by saying that if Father Sorin had been a businessman, everything he had done would make perfect sense; but since he was a religious and under obedience, his conduct was therefore unjustifiable. What they seemed to overlook was that it was the duty of a religious entrusted with the temporal affairs of his community to administer them like a zealous and prudent businessman and that it was their duty as the top authority in the Congregation to support him when he did so.

Father Sorin had little patience for what he regarded as old-country pettiness and shortsightedness, and he usually said so with more candor than delicacy. Sometimes, on the contrary, he apologized for his behavior and promised amendment. But whether his words were contrite or unrepentant, his deeds remained the same. He went on building, amassing debts, neglecting to submit accounts to the mother house, pledging its credit without authority or even notice.

In February 1845, Bishop de la Hailandièrc was at Le Mans, and Father Moreau and he worked out a formula which resolved nothing. The agreement they signed recognized the dependence on Sainte-Croix of the foundations in the diocese of Vincennes, "while still regarding the worthy bishop as their local superior." Perhaps they thought they were imposing two sets of controls on Father Sorin, for the bishop too had his problems with him. To protect themselves further, they agreed that no houses would be established outside the diocese without the bishop's written consent.

All of this Father Moreau spelled out for Father Sorin, repeating his explicit prohibition against founding houses or undertaking extraordinary expenditures without advance approval. To soften the blow, he freed the American houses from the obligation of repaying the mother house for training their brothers and sisters, while reserving the right to impose a special levy later, should circumstances demand. And he recalled their duty to send yearly financial reports.

Father Sorin accepted the benefits as a matter of right and ignored the limitations. Bishop de la Hailandière was hurt when he saw that the clause recognizing him as local superior was a dead letter, and his suspicions increased each time he learned of a new move by Father Sorin to establish a foundation outside the diocese. The two were also poles apart in their concept of the educational function of Notre Dame. Father Sorin planned to teach youth from all parts of the country in a high-class school. The bishop's concern was his immediate need for instructors of converts and primary teachers for the children of the poor.

Father Moreau finally ordered Father Sorin to come to Le Mans for the general chapter of 1846 to iron things out. Once these two met face to face, they had not much difficulty in making each other understand the inevitability of the position each had adopted. There was then little the chapter could do but bury the past after a postmortem that cannot have been too satisfactory from its viewpoint.

For the moment the chapter seemed to accept defeat generously. It wiped out nearly all Father Sorin's outstanding debt to the mother house, and it gave him additional helpers, three priests, three brothers, and six sisters. But it went on to repeat all the restrictions already in force, and this Father Sorin regarded as a personal affront. He took what they offered, then went right back to his old ways, continuing to make his own decisions, confiding only in those who shared his ideas, confusing the accounts and misleading the council, arrogating to himself the powers of the superior general, blaming his errors on the mother house when things went wrong.

In Canada, things were developing differently. The superior at St. Laurent was a Father Louis Vérité, a man of God with an overwhelming thirst for perfection, but very gentle and lacking the firmness desirable in a leader. He was delighted when, after a visit from Father Drouelle, sent from France to report on the American houses, Father Joseph Rézé was chosen to replace him.

The new superior was a more vigorous type—honest, firm, straightforward—and he soon put the foundation on the solid footing on which it remained for the many years of his rule. In this he was but carrying out the express instructions of Father Moreau. When Father Drouelle reported that the brothers who had recently come to St. Laurent from France had lost the spirit of obedience, were careless in rising and in their spiritual exercises, and were disrespectful to their superior, Father Moreau told Father Rézé that his first duty was to re-establish a true religious spirit and that he would have him abandon Canada rather than remain on any other condition.

Canada, therefore, followed a rhythm of development closer to that of France. There was not the abrupt change which in Father Sorin seemed to develop a new man with new characteristics, and as a result an emotional gulf developed between Notre Dame and St. Laurent. The Canadians felt the Americans had abandoned the spirit and methods of Holy Cross, while the Americans were sure that the community at St. Laurent had not grasped the significance of the New World and consequently would never get anywhere in it.

Father Drouelle was soon made aware of the difference. The first part of his mission had been most successful. St. Laurent welcomed him, recognized his authority, and submitted to the reorganization he imposed in the name of the superior general. But his major task lay ahead. Father Moreau's principal purpose in sending a visitor was to make a working agreement with the United States houses, to have Father Sorin recognize the authority of the superior general and the general council and abide by regulations, in particular to follow their system of financial accounting and to repay overdue debts before starting new ventures.

Father Drouelle spent three most enjoyable months at Notre Dame and wrote long detailed accounts of his impressions to Father Moreau. He was astonished at the tremendous progress made in a few years, he reported, the prosperous farm, the schools, the community buildings for men and women, the Indian missions. He had praise for everything and for everyone, except Americans in general. The twelve novices in the brothers' novitiate were for the greater part Irish, pious men of deep faith. Almost all of the sisters' fifteen novices were also Irish, and as edifying as Carthusians. "As for the Americans, converting them to the religious life would require a miracle of grace similar to that which hurled St. Paul to the ground."

The general council at Sainte-Croix was likely not too pleased at the enthusiastic reports on Father Sorin's work, especially as they were interspersed with suggestions that France could have done much more than it had done to help him. But whether they liked them or not, these were the principal results they obtained from Father Drouelle's visit. He carried out none of the assignments they had entrusted to him.

Father Sorin, for his part, did not change. It was about this time that he sent several brothers to California to prospect for gold, of course without notifying either France or the bishop of Vincennes. It was the height of the gold rush, and undoubtedly he was gambling on a lucky strike to solve his financial problems. In his unpublished history of the establishment of Holy Cross in America, a work which at times presents events as he would have liked them to occur rather than as they actually occurred, he offers a different motivation.

A brother had recently left the community, he said, and was threatening to establish himself with a wife in the immediate neighborhood. To prevent this scandal, Father Sorin agreed to underwrite the cost of an expedition to California for the ex-brother, three brothers from Notre Dame, and three other young men of the district. He would receive in return not only the entire share of the brothers' profits but half the profits of the others.

Unfortunately, they found no gold. Still worse, one of the brothers perished in the wilderness without the last sacraments. Once again, Father Sorin had failed to obtain Father Moreau's permission beforehand. He himself claimed only that he had written a report after the expedition had set out but that this letter never reached its destination. When the news reached Sainte-Croix much later through a third party, it inevitably hardened the views of those who disapproved of Father Sorin's methods. It is proper to add, nevertheless, that Father Moreau wrote to Father Cointet that, after receiving Father Sorin's explanations, he no longer condemned his intentions.

The Society for the Propagation of the Faith was also worried about the extent of his spending. It had been sending him substantial sums, but he was forever clamoring for more. Father Moreau, who acted as intermediary, reported to him that the Society "does not understand how so much money can disappear."

In 1851, Father Sorin again visited France, and the general council went over the same ground once more. The result was the same. It reaffirmed the decisions to limit his authority. But once he was back in America, everything resumed its normal course.

Father Moreau now attempted a rather daring but imaginative way out of the dilemma. He had reached the conclusion that the simplest way to establish normality would be to remove Father Sorin from the American scene. He did not, however, want to humiliate him publicly. He recognized that his personality and contacts were an integral element in the reputation and financial credit of the Congregation in the United States, just as were his own in France. Any withdrawal of confidence could have dangerous repercussions. The complex of buildings and activities at Notre Dame might be a sound investment (as time proved it to be), but what would it bring in a bankruptcy sale in 1850 if creditors suddenly pressed for payment?

Halfway round the world, Father Moreau saw what he hoped might be the solution. The Holy See had told him that the superior of his band of missionaries in East Bengal would be designated vicar-apostolic and consecrated bishop as soon as a see was established. It was the most significant honor so far rewarded to Holy Cross. If only Father Sorin would accept.

But Father Sorin would have nothing to do with East Bengal. I am unworthy to become a bishop, he insisted, an understandable and praiseworthy attitude if it was not supported by a torrent of protests from himself and his sympathizers that Notre Dame was his and needed him. Father Moreau had to find another superior for the Bengal mission.

To make matters worse, a new source of major friction developed. Father Sorin claimed jurisdiction over all foundations in North America, and certainly over all in the United States. This claim had never been admitted by Father Moreau or the general chapter. On the contrary, they treated Canada as a separate unit depending directly on the mother house, and they similarly regarded New Orleans, founded directly from France and operating in the very different society of the old South.

In the exercise of his asserted authority, Father Sorin refused to accept as superior of the house in New Orleans a Father Gouësse whom Father Moreau had confirmed in that position, and he notified both the brothers there and the Archbishop that Father Gouësse was no longer "recognized as one of our own." Father Gouësse left for France without a protest, but the General Chapter of August 1851, overriding Father Moreau's opposition, decided to teach Father Sorin a lesson, and sent Father Gouësse back to New Orleans. To this quite proper exercise of the supreme authority of the Congregation, Father Sorin reacted as to a declaration of war. He sent a formal order to Father Gouësse to leave the country, and, when this was ignored, he assembled the Notre Dame chapters of the three branches of Holy Cross—fathers, brothers, and sisters—and had them record their intention of withdrawing from the Congregation for a trial period of five years, though continuing to live as religious.

Widespread confusion followed. Father Sorin waved the document threateningly at the heads of Father Moreau and the general council in France to show how determined and united the entire American group was. What did not emerge for some time was that nobody outside the chapter had ever been told. And however bold a face they presented to the mother house, the chapter members were unhappy about their canonical status and submitted an explanation to the Archbishop of Cincinnati, and to Canon Heurtebize back at Le Mans, whom all regarded as elder statesman and adviser to Holy Cross. They were very upset when both disapproved the action.

The bishop of Vincennes also counseled prudence and urged that a final decision should be postponed until after a delegate arrived from Sainte-Croix. He added, however, that he would not let Notre Dame disappear, but would rather dispense them from their vows if its existence was threatened. Father Sorin grasped this statement as a full justification, ignoring the reservations.

The Archbishop of New Orleans urged Father Moreau to come himself to America to iron out the situation. He agreed in principle but pleaded that he was swamped with urgent problems at home. The political situation in France was, as always, precarious. Living costs were rising rapidly. The Roman foundation claimed much attention, especially as each indication of progress increased the hope of getting the coveted papal approval. And relations with Bishop Bouvier were very bad.

Reluctantly, Father Moreau sent Father Chappé in his stead to make peace in America. The details were handled without haste, hoping that time might dissipate some of the heat. Father Chappé stopped off first in Canada and found everything in excellent shape. Meanwhile, a special committee, formed at Le Mans to study the situation, completed its report, which was a condemnation of Father Sorin. It instructed Father Chappé to use his judgment but recommended that he make "a stern example" to prevent recurrence of the scandal.

The list of charges, as formulated in a letter from Father Drouelle to Father Sorin about this time, was a formidable one. It included the recruitment of subjects in France and the advice to them to have nothing to do with the mother house; the expedition to California; circulars sent out by Father Sorin and expressed in terms which made him sound like a superior general; changes in the habit; a declaration of insubordination when those at Notre Dame felt themselves strong enough to win their independence, and the distortion of the current situation in order to appear as victims.

When the visitor arrived at Notre Dame on September 7, 1853, Father Sorin and the local chapters took a strong stand, insisting that their action had withdrawn them from the jurisdiction of Holy Cross. Father Chappé might stay "as a friend" as long as he liked, but they denied his authority to make decisions or issue orders. When, however, he wanted to get the views of the community, he learned with amazement that the withdrawal was an absolute secret. Nobody outside the chapters knew anything of its decision to sever relations.

This bombshell changed everything. Should he take the responsibility of revealing the schism, perhaps precipitating desertions and certainly causing scandal? He decided that Father Sorin's mind was not as finally made up as he pretended and that his own best move was to continue the secret negotiations. After many extraordinary changes of attitude, Father Sorin one day capitulated completely. He himself described his change of heart as "miraculous" and said it occurred while he was saying the rosary. In any case he signed a formal retractation and the action of the local chapters was rescinded. Father Chappé returned in triumph to France with the documents.

The general council would not let Father Sorin off so lightly. It made him come to Le Mans to submit in person and then demoted him to assistant head of the American foundations under Father Rézé. It agreed, however, to continue his role as local superior of Notre Dame, and since the Notre Dame complex was the biggest and most dynamic element of Holy Cross in North America, he retained a position of great strength.

Prospects now looked bright, but unfortunately a series of minor incidents created a new crisis. As a conciliatory gesture to Father Sorin, the mother house decided to move Father Gouësse from New Orleans to Canada and sent a Father Gastineau to succeed him. Father Gastineau, a very impressionable man, traveled first to Notre Dame and delayed there much longer than planned. Just what they told him is not recorded, but his volatile nature made him an ideal subject for brainwashing; and he no sooner arrived in New Orleans than he became terrified of his assignment and fled to Canada.

The story got around among the clergy, and when it reached Father Sorin he exploded and demanded an apology of Father Moreau for exposing him to public ridicule by sending unsuitable subjects to America.

Father Moreau tried hard to find another superior for New Orleans, but a series of deaths extended the hiatus. Finally, Father Gouësse (still the acting superior) and his local chapter asked the general council to abandon the house, saying that Father Sorin had made it impossible to continue. The Archbishop of New Orleans sympathized with them, but his concern was to save the foundation, and he begged Father Moreau and Father Sorin to resolve their differences.

Father Moreau wrote Father Sorin a magnanimous letter, burying the past and appealing to his generosity to take the action which only he could take to save New Orleans. The letter must have arrived on a bad day, for the answer reflected only Father Sorin's least attractive qualities. What is interesting is its development of the idea of spheres of influence. Any houses in America not under Notre Dame were its "enemies," and accordingly New Orleans must depend exclusively on Notre Dame or cease to exist. "I refuse," he summed up his position, "unless I am absolute master."

Father Moreau would not be baited. His reply, phrased with characteristic gentleness, confined itself to announcing that he was finally able to come and see for himself.

That was January 1855, but the visit did not take place for two and a half years. Things were desperate in France. Living costs had skyrocketed, aggravating financial difficulties to such an extent that Father Moreau was turning down all postulants and thinking of closing the novitiate. It was also the year of the great spiritual crisis, when (as he himself put it) he wrestled with the devil and for long periods saw himself tottering on the brink of hell.

There were also the time-consuming negotiations for papal approval of the Constitutions, a goal reached only in 1855 after Bishop Bouvier's death in 1854, and then only for the priests and brothers. Failure to win approval for the sisters not only necessitated much revision both of rules and administration but it raised new tensions everywhere, especially in America.

Father Moreau's visit was accordingly postponed from one month to another, but the problems requiring his attention did not stand still. Provisional solutions had to be found. The Archbishop of New Orleans had installed a Father Raymond, a French Sulpician, in the orphanage to hold it together until Holy Cross should send a new superior. Father Raymond had known Father

Moreau in France, and on the latter's advice had selected New Orleans when he decided to take a group of French priests and seminarians to work in American mission territories. He soon saw the value of the contribution being made by the Holy Cross religious in New Orleans, and urged Father Moreau to listen to the Archbishop's repeated appeals and find a way to continue.

Father Moreau agreed not to decide the issue before his own arrival, and he presented a compromise intended to placate Father Sorin without prejudicing the principle that divided them. He would send a superior from Holy Cross and an assistant superior from Notre Dame, the house to be attached temporarily to the Notre Dame province, with the understanding that it would form a separate province as soon as possible.

Father Sorin offered no immediate criticism. He had already, after a short demotion, been restored as provincial, and now his authority over New Orleans was reaffirmed. It would be soon enough to take up the cudgels if a change was later attempted. It seemed more immediately important to build up Notre Dame itself, so he offered a reorganization of the Congregation of Holy Cross based on the political system of the United States, as he understood it. The provinces, he proposed, should be autonomous in regard to all decisions except those that might have repercussions on the entire Congregation.

Father Moreau took the unusual proposal very calmly. He said he could accept it as a basis for relations between the Notre Dame province and the mother house, but he expressly excluded Canada and New Orleans. Father Sorin as usual, noted the favorable part of the decision and ignored the rest.

The new superior sent by France to New Orleans proved no more acceptable to Father Sorin than his predecessors. While the Archbishop of New Orleans had nothing but praise for Father Guesdon's material and spiritual administration, Father Sorin peppered the mother house with complaints. It did not, however, prove necessary to act on them, for an outbreak of yellow fever intervened in September 1855, carrying off the New Orleans superior and several colleagues.

News of this disaster reached Father Moreau at the peak of the spiritual crisis mentioned earlier, adding to his belief that his lifework was in process of disintegration. He was obsessed with the fear that his creditors would call for payment and bankrupt Holy Cross, and in anticipation he appealed to the American Houses to help. Canada was penniless, and New Orleans could raise only a small sum. Father Sorin, however, reacted with the generosity which characterized his better moments. He replied at once that he would of course raise the fifteen thousand francs requested and authorized Father Moreau to issue a draft on him for that amount with thirty days' notice, adding that he would shortly be able to contribute a second fifteen thousand francs. Very soon, however, he withdrew his offer and demanded immediate repayment of the first fifteen thousand, which had already changed hands, saying that he was outraged by the New Orleans community because it had given scant welcome to his delegate and wanted to remain under the mother house.

Approval by Rome on May 13, 1857, of the Congregation of Holy Cross, after a long series of hesitations to be detailed shortly, provoked a new outburst of dissatisfaction at Notre Dame. The sisters in the United States represented a much greater part of the operation than they did in France. Consequently, while France had rejoiced at the approval for the fathers and brothers, the local council at Notre Dame was plunged into grief by the decision to postpone action on the sisters. It ruled that it dare not even risk announcing the news and accordingly withheld the superior general's circular from the community.

A new clash developed in August 1855, from the request of the Archbishop of New York for sisters for an orphanage, which stipulated that the foundation should remain directly dependent on France. The offer was attractive, not only because it introduced Holy Cross to New York, but because the archdiocese would underwrite all costs and had ambitious development plans. In deference to Father Sorin, Father Moreau tried to soften the conditions. The mother house, he proposed, would control New York "through the intermediary of the Provincial at Notre Dame."

The Archbishop was adamant. Notre Dame would have no place in the project. This was too much for Father Sorin. He sent Mother Angela to New York to "examine the situation," and on her recommendation he ordered the house closed. While the sisters were being dispersed, a delegate of Father Moreau arrived from Le Mans and attempted to countermand the order. The clash became so acute that the Archbishop had to intervene, closing the house down immediately in the interest of peace.

One might wonder what energies could remain for the work to which they were all formally dedicated. Nevertheless, that work prospered amazingly. Father Sorin's report at the end of 1856 records the statistics. The province of Notre Dame had 18 houses, with 238 religious, of whom 18 were Salvatorists, 80 Josephites, and 140 Marianites. They were educating three thousand children. The total of houses and personnel, he noted, was fully a third higher than a year earlier. Notre Dame had accordingly, one-fourth of all the priests and brothers, and more than half the sisters, and it was educating nearly a third of all the children entrusted to the care of Holy Cross throughout the world.

The administration of Notre Dame sent a sister to Le Mans to express its grievances to the general council in January 1857. After hearing all complaints, Father Moreau and the Council insisted on the papal order separating the sisters from the other two communities, placing them exclusively under his authority. He said that any who were unwilling to conform were free to leave; they would be expelled if they did not submit. He also examined once more all the financial dealings, about which Notre Dame constantly complained, and struck a balance, forbidding further discussion.

The sister delegate called for the return of the fifteen thousand francs which Father Sorin had sent in 1855 in response to Father Moreau's urgent appeal. Father Moreau agreed to recognize this "gift" as a loan, but insisted that the amount Father Sorin had earlier admitted as owed by him to Holy Cross should be credited against it. At the same time, Father Moreau expressed extreme dissatisfaction with the whole temporal administration of the Indiana province. Notre Dame was furious at all this, resenting a reminder that substantial former debts had been canceled and also the insistence that the balance admitted by Father Sorin in 1846 should be repaid. Instead, it called for repayment in full of its recent "gift."

There is, perhaps, little point in wondering if an earlier visit to America by the superior general might not have radically altered the development of the Congregation in the new world. What is certain is that Father Moreau himself was always anxious to make the trip and that the reasons holding him back had been sound ones.

Finally, however, the moment arrived when he could get away. The conventual church at the mother house had been completed and consecrated. Rome had approved the Constitutions. The political situation in France was not more than normally confused. He booked passage on the *S. S. Fulton* and sailed from Le Havre in July 1857.

As he crossed the ocean, Father Moreau thought less about himself than about the many members of his family who had sailed to various parts of the world to distant missions. The story of the growth of Holy Cross was already an impressive one. Figures compiled a year earlier showed that it numbered 72 priests, 322 brothers, and 254 sisters. Its 114 houses included 86 primary schools, 8 high schools, and 4 boarding schools.

From its foundation, it had been given many evidences of favor and esteem by the Holy See, indulgences and privileges for the Association of St. Joseph and the Good Shepherd, its own Ordo and calendar, the right to celebrate the Feast of the Sacred Heart as its "titular feast," special faculties to erect the Way of the Cross, and plenary indulgences for its students on specified feasts. The Pope placed Holy Cross in charge of his own orphanage in

Rome. The Congregation For the Propagation of the Faith had entrusted a mission to it in Bengal. And to crown all, Rome had finally approved the Constitutions.

Everywhere they lived in great poverty, for the rapid expansion involved huge expenditures which had to be met from donations and from the current income produced by the schools and other activities. But the financial situation was basically sound. A year earlier Father Moreau had made a detailed report in which he could state that current debts had always been paid and would continue to be paid. Assets of the mother house had grown in twenty-five years from under five thousand francs to 1,200,000, this despite the fact that it had contributed substantial sums to the development of the many foundations in different countries.

True, there were problems, like those now requiring his presence in America, but they were the problems of life, growth, and enthusiasm. Nowhere did the Congregation offer brighter promise than in the New World. There, as in Europe, its members were progressing in the religious life, and they had a like devotion to work and study.

The primary purpose of Father Moreau's visit was to complete the separation of the sisters from the other branches of Holy Cross, a condition imposed by Rome when approving the Constitutions of the priests and brothers. In Montreal, his first stop after spending a day in New York, the formalities were carried out without a hitch. He confirmed Father Rézé as vicar for Canada and canonically installed the local superiors of the priests and brothers, as well as the superioress of the sisters. Property was divided equally between the two communities, and so were liabilities. Everywhere there was rejoicing at his presence, and all his decisions were received with pleasure. As one of the sisters remarked, "Our Very Reverend Father could tear the house down and no one would say a word."

At Notre Dame, the going was not so smooth. Certainly the formal welcome, with ringing of bells and processions of the students and orphans, was no less effusive than that of Canada. Nor was there any question of a direct challenge to his authority, such as had occurred earlier. But beneath the surface there remained deep divergences of viewpoint, which Father Moreau felt compelled to recognize by glossing over points that Notre Dame interpreted differently from the mother house. His approach was, as always, that of a father with his children. So long as he was satisfied that they meant well, he could wait patiently and count on time to change attitudes. But he did not deceive himself as to the existence of problems.

"Here again I had many occasions to thank our Lord for the spirit of faith, the winning simplicity, and the admirable docility with which all opened their hearts to me and received my words of advice," he wrote about this visit while aboard ship on his way home. "Meanwhile, the enemy of good was on the alert, and I felt as if some invisible force were working against me. I encountered a mysterious kind of stubborn opposition from this bitter enemy of all God's works."

The open opposition centered mainly on the separation of the sisters, and just what was decided is far from clear. Father Sorin's unpublished diary describes the founder's visit in glowing terms. He organized the local chapters, he said, doing the work of several months in a few weeks, and doing everything well. Finally, he "arranged the separation of the finances of the sisters from those of the other two societies."

Father Moreau's account, while less specific, seems to confirm this. The meetings with the sisters, he wrote, lasting sometimes until very late at night, produced their fruit, "and all the difficulties which had remained unsettled until then were arranged by mutual agreement, thanks to the conciliatory and generous attitude of Father Sorin and his councilors."

Perhaps both parties thought at the time that they were in agreement, but later events showed this not to be the case. It seems certain that there was no physical division of assets and liabilities, as had been effected in Canada. Perhaps they reached agreement on some kind of formula for a division, but if so, nothing was put in writing. Later, the matter would again become an occasion of misunderstandings. The general chapter would accuse Father Sorin of separating the temporalities of the sisters on his own initiative and without authority, while he would answer with a tone of resigned exasperation that Father Moreau had settled the entire matter while at Notre Dame and that he was an innocent bystander.

Another major point of difference concerned the control of the sisters. Rome had ruled that Father Moreau was to be their superior until such time as their Constitutions should be approved, and while he was in Canada, he had appointed Mother Mary of the Seven Dolors as superior general until a general chapter could be held. It will be recalled, however, that the bishop of Le Mans had always refused to recognize the sisters as constituting a religious congregation and that the first canonical foundation was that made by Father Sorin. Notre Dame consequently considered itself the mother house of the Marianites, and the sisters there could not understand how the mother general could reside anywhere else.

Again Father Moreau sought a compromise. He did not revoke his previous decision, but he urged Mother Mary of the Seven Dolors not to describe herself as mother general. The compromise may have avoided greater harm at the time, but it did not achieve a lasting understanding among the sisters. In the end, they developed into three separate congregations, with the mother house of the first in France, of the second in Canada, and of the third in Indiana. Thus they have remained to the present time.

CHAPTER ELEVEN

Trial and Division in France

"I encountered a mysterious kind of stubborn opposition from the bitter enemy of all God's works," Father Moreau had written about one experience in America. The same comment applied to much that was happening during those same years in France.

Elements of pettiness, meanness, and self-seeking on the part of some of the principals cannot be entirely ruled out. But, by and large, the people involved were honorable men with high motives. They had pledged their lives to God's service, and they were trying seriously to promote the kingdom of God. What they did makes no sense unless viewed in the framework in which Father Moreau did in fact view it: as the work of the devil enraged by the good this group was doing and permitted by God to use his preternatural powers to the full.

What the devil never learns is that not only can he not win, but that he actually advances God's work. Shaken to its foundations, Holy Cross survived the crisis. It grew to adult stature and condition, no longer needing the constant protection of one individual to maintain it.

For Father Moreau himself the test was equally extreme. It was the testing of Job. He was stripped of everything he held dear. His children rejected him. He was found guilty of the defects most foreign to his nature—self-seeking, craftiness, duplicity, disobedience. He seemed abandoned by God. But through everything he retained his sublime faith and confidence.

The first episode had occurred in 1855, two years before his visit to America. It had the characteristics of the mystical experience which spiritual writers call the dark night of the soul, and it is so interpreted by those who have studied it.

All through that summer Father Moreau endured a genuine spiritual crisis. He could see only the negative aspects of his situation: fifteen years waiting for approval of his society, deepening hostility of his bishop, dissension within his family striking at the principle of authority, activities in Africa drastically curtailed, the best of the missionaries sent to Bengal dead, epidemics of yellow fever decimating the foundations in New Orleans, living costs shooting up in France. In addition, he was in poor physical shape and had lost almost completely the use of one eye.

Although a report he had recently submitted was satisfactory, he became obsessed with the idea that Holy Cross was bankrupt. "I haven't the courage to write you," he wrote Father Drouelle in Rome. "I am afraid of collapsing under the weight of our debts." Coupled with this was a conviction that the perennially unstable French government would be overthrown by violence and be replaced by one even more hostile to religion. "Everyone fears," he wrote, "that a revolution is just around the corner."

The climax came in August. He thought he saw the impending ruin of the Congregation and took steps to wind up its affairs. He suspended the building of the church and the mother house, cut out all but the most essential expenditures, let the hired help go, instructed all members of the Congregation in France to get together what each would need when the catastrophe struck, sent postulants back to their homes, even refused money gifts on the ground that the donors would not offer them if they knew that Holy Cross was about to fold. The routine functioning of the community continued only because the bursar forced him to sign papers by physically controlling the movement of his hand.

Like Job, he suffered all the anguish of despair, but also like Job he refused to despair. As he told one of his colleagues, the devil appeared and taunted him. "You are damned, Moreau," he jeered, "and all the religious under your direction will be damned too."

Through everything he continued to pray, even though God hid Himself and Father Moreau's pleadings seemed to drop into the void. At night, while all slept, he kept vigil in the chapel. "I went from station to station," he said,

> searching for light, for an inspiration, and I found nothing, absolutely nothing. I knocked on the tabernacle door. I waited and received no answer, not the least encouragement. At that moment I understood something of our Lord's abandonment in His agony. . . .
> I then understood perfectly the suicide of Judas.

The trial passed as mysteriously as it had come. After about two months of suffering, he received a letter from a lady who said she saw him in the same state as Peter walking on the water. The apparently chance reference flooded his soul with light. His confidence returned as he realized that the same power in fact sustained him as that which enabled Peter to walk on the waves.

One inevitably wonders if such an experience is not a form of mental illness. In fact, some interpreted it so at the time. "The rumor was spread abroad that I was insane," Father Moreau wrote. "Nothing could be more false. I was just as calm as I am today, and I enjoyed the use of all my faculties." Experts in the fields of psychiatry and mystical theology, who have examined the evidence, agree. Despite superficial similarities, the two sets of phenomena are sharply different, and in this case they conclude that what Father Moreau experienced was truly a mystical experience intended by God to purify a chosen soul and purge it of any vestige of attachment to worldly things. This diagnosis seems confirmed by subsequent events which stripped him progressively of everything he had achieved and to which he reacted not as a neurotic but as a holy man.

But before the final humiliation, there was to be one supreme satisfaction, when the Holy See placed the stamp of its formal approval on the Congregation of Holy Cross.

As already indicated, Bishop Bouvier died while visiting Rome at the end of December 1854. His death did not automatically ensure the coveted papal endorsement, but it swept away the one major obstacle. It was now possible to put the machinery in motion.

The following March, the Congregation of Propaganda nominated a canonist, Father Secchi-Murro, a Servite, to examine the Rules of the Congregation. In June, the Sacred Congregation studied his report and authorized the Decree of Praise, but in a limited form. Even this limited decree was not issued, since it had first to be approved by the Pope, and he was unwilling to do so unless the Rules were amended to affect a complete legal separation of the sisters from the two other groups. He was ready to approve the priests and brothers, he said, but he did not want sisters in the community.

Father Moreau was deeply committed to the concept of a threefold society including sisters on equal terms with priests and brothers. He was, nevertheless, far more committed to acceptance of whatever the Pope might decide, and he immediately declared that he would welcome papal approval of the priests and brothers, even though no decision was made as regards the sisters.

Father Secchi-Murro had also raised some questions concerning minor provisions of the Rules, especially as regards government of the community, and the general chapter, which met in August 1855, approved modifications to meet his reservations. There was nothing now to do but wait.

In the spring of 1856, Father Moreau went once more to Rome to add his personal appeal to that of his representatives there. He carried with him a letter from Bishop Nanquette of Le Mans, who had been consecrated and enthroned the previous November, in which his new bishop expressed to the Congregation of Propaganda his support of all of Father Moreau's undertakings. The Congregation of Holy Cross, he wrote, had been founded and developed in the midst of countless obstacles. It had nevertheless succeeded in the temporal order in placing itself on a solid foundation, and on the spiritual side it gave proof of being animated with a genuinely religious spirit and with filial devotion to the Holy See. As a teaching and apostolic congregation, it had rendered great services, and with the approbation of the Holy See it would be able to render even more.

This was the one essential document that had heretofore been lacking in the dossier. As for the sisters, Father Moreau repeated that he was ready to make any sacrifice that the Holy Father desired. Pius IX, for his part, stressed that he was not opposed to them as such. "You will govern them separately," he told Father Moreau. "I bless them too, and later you can submit their rules to the Sacred Congregation."

On this occasion, as previously, the Pope gave Father Moreau many evidences of his personal esteem, leading him to believe that everything was settled in his favor. He did not, however, understand all the delays and formalities surrounding an official act of a Roman congregation. Although Propaganda met in April and considered his request, no decision was announced, and he was forced to leave Rome once more with empty hands.

There were several reasons for the last-minute hesitation of the Sacred Congregation. Some of the Cardinals had themselves seen Holy Cross at work in Vigna Pia and had concluded that all the brothers were either farmers or artisans. They could not understand how workmen could be equal partners with priests in a Congregation, and Father Moreau had to repeat his explanation of the scope and function of the brothers. In addition, Cardinal Prefect Franzoni had died, leaving the Congregation of Propaganda without a head. And on top of all this, they did not share Father Moreau's sense of haste. On the contrary, it was never the Sacred Congregation's practice to decide in a hurry. The Christian Brothers were founded in 1680 but received papal approval only in 1724, five years after their founder's death. The Holy Ghost Fathers waited from 1703 to 1821; the Daughters of Wisdom, from 1703 to 1753. The Sacred Congregation moved at its own rhythm, so that the decree was approved on May 19, 1856, and confirmed by Pius IX a week later. Here is the text:

> Praise is due this Institute consisting of priests and brothers, who are nevertheless to be so united among themselves in friendly union that, while preserving the nature of each society, neither one may dominate the other but that both may cooperate in the best possible manner in the attainment of their respective ends. Let it not be easy for the Brothers of St. Joseph to be promoted to the priesthood.

In the same month of May 1856, Father Moreau, in a circular letter, touched on some of the points which he considered significant in the life of the Congregation and its members. He noted that the body had grown rapidly; but the body had meaning and life only in so far as it had a soul; and its soul could be nothing else than the spirit of regularity, the observance of the vows, and perseverance in one's vocation, "which is weakened and lost only by negligence and disregard for our Rules."

Only second to the importance of a spiritual life, Father Moreau went on, was a spirit of work and study. This was a subject he frequently touched upon, for he sought to develop his communities into true intellectual centers. That, he said, was why he was so happy about the foundation of St. Bridget's in Rome, where he proposed to assemble the Congregation's most promising students for graduate work in philosophy, theology, and canon law.

For the brothers in charge of schools he also sketched a program of study to deepen their knowledge and perfect their teaching methods. He praised particularly those brothers who had written textbooks and urged others to imitate them. He himself, he said, was completing a book on teaching methods intended to achieve more uniformity in the Congregation's schools. It was, in fact, published that same year, and it reveals a quite extraordinary understanding of the skills and attitudes which made a good teacher. It stresses a positive approach, which can be summed up in the principle that the teacher must look for the fine qualities latent in the young mind.

Less than a year later, the Decree of Praise was complemented by a further important act of the Sacred Congregation. A decree dated May 13, 1857, approved the Rules and Constitutions. Father Moreau immediately announced the glad news in a brief circular. After simply quoting the telegram from Father Drouelle, he added these few words: "Upon receipt of this letter, you will recite the *Te Deum*, will celebrate, or have celebrated, a Mass of Thanksgiving, and will read your Rules in their entirety for spiritual reading."

The telegram had arrived at a most opportune moment, for the consecration of the mother church had already been set for the following June 17. Despite everything, Father Moreau had persisted tenaciously and had finally achieved what he had sought, a spacious and beautiful church that would be the visible center, the unifying image of his three communities, the symbol of souls joined together as living stones in a spiritual edifice for the glory of God.

Cardinal Donnet, Archbishop of Bordeaux, presided at the ceremonies, surrounded by eight bishops, the abbot of Solesmes, the prefect of the department and its military commander, and a vast throng of notables and unknowns from far and near. The ceremony lasted six hours, the entire liturgy as prescribed by the rubrics being chanted by the community. Among the many spiritual benefits Father Moreau had gained from his friendship with Dom Guéranger, the abbot of nearby Solesmes, was a dedication to liturgical chant, which was already prescribed for use in all houses of the Congregation. It had become a feature of the mother church. Bishop Nanquette celebrated the Pontifical Mass. The Cardinal Archbishop preached.

It should have been a perfect day for Father Moreau. It was almost perfect. And yet it was marred by an outrageous public humiliation which deserves a place here only because it demonstrates the bitterness and obstinacy of the opposition to the founder, and because it provides an anticipation of what still lay ahead for him.

Bishop Nanquette, now bishop of Le Mans, had made generous amends for his predecessor's treatment of Father Moreau by his eloquent appeal to Rome in favor of Holy Cross. But among his clergy there were some who had sided with Bishop Bouvier, and one of these was the diocesan master of ceremonies. He agreed to the bishop's request to direct the function, but only on condition that Father Moreau should not appear at any moment during the ceremony.

Since it was impossible to get along without a master of ceremonies, they dispensed with the man who had built the church and created the work of which it was the symbol. Throughout the ceremony he remained in a balcony in the transept, with the invited members of the laity.

More serious incidents, inspired by equally petty motives, were soon to follow. One of these was a lawsuit, which was already being prepared, and which would drag on for years and do incalculable harm. The sister of a Canon Dubignon, a close friend of Father Moreau, had left him a valuable estate, spelling out in specific terms in her will that she did not want this property to go to her niece under any circumstances. The niece, nevertheless, contested the will, alleging that it was vitiated by a secret trust in favor of Holy Cross. In addition, she charged forgery and undue influence.

Father Moreau was outraged by the injustice of the charges and decided to defend. Passions ran high. The girl had influence, and she even succeeded in getting several priests to testify that the legatee was an individual undeterred by scruples.

The court took little time to toss out the charges of undue influence and forgery. But it probed deeply into the question of a secret trust. The anticlerical laws were insistent that no property should be left to a nonauthorized religious organization, and since Father Moreau was Holy Cross, it was easy to argue that what went to him went to it.

After long hesitation, the court decided that the will was valid, and a great sigh of relief went up from Holy Cross. But the comfort was short-lived. Father Moreau was typically generous in victory. He offered to pay all costs if the other party would accept the decision as final. His enemies, however, would not yield. Relying on prejudice to override justice, they went to the court of appeals. It reversed the judgment, and the supreme court upheld the reversal.

During the four years the case had dragged on, many things had happened to increase the destructive impact of this blow, which altered radically the balance of Father Moreau's accounts. He accepted the decision calmly as the will of God, but he did not hide from himself the leverage it would give his enemies both external and internal. For it had by now become apparent that a serious challenge to his administration had developed even within Holy Cross itself.

The leaders of this movement were some of the most distinguished members of the congregation, men picked by Father Moreau for positions of top authority and prestige—Father Drouelle, the procurator at Rome and liaison with the Holy See, Father Champeau, superior of Paris and head of its important college, and Father Sorin, founder and head of Holy Cross in the United States. Their motives and objectives were very mixed, and one cannot dismiss them as simply selfish or unworthy. Certain incidents were undoubtedly shameful, but one must recognize that those involved were in general well intentioned. The ultimate causes are as mysterious as those of Father Moreau's recent spiritual experience.

Certain changes had, however, occurred which facilitated the development of this opposition. As already noted, the canonist named by the Congregation of Propaganda in 1855 had recommended modifications in the Constitutions to correct a tendency to undue concentration of authority in the hands of the superior general, and the general chapter of that year made the desired changes. The general chapter of June 1857 introduced another special constitution to deal with the organization of the program of studies, also added at Rome's request. Canonically speaking the papal approval applied only to the Constitutions. The Rules, which supplemented and explained them, constituting a kind of commentary and a spiritual and practical adaptation of their general provisions to the needs of daily life, derived their authority from the general chapter. The approval of the Constitutions, nevertheless, also necessitated various changes in the Rules, and the Superior General felt that all these amendments to both the Constitutions and the Rules should be rapidly implemented, and that all their provisions should be enforced more strictly than before.

When, however, he began to apply this policy, the intermediate superiors resented and resisted the attempts to curb their discretion. They found it all too easy to give themselves credit for the previous progress and to feel that the superior general's new insistence on obedience was the petulance of an old man who had fulfilled his function but could not see that it was time for him to hand over control to younger and more progressive leaders.

Father Moreau's visit to America took place during the months immediately following the consecration of the mother church, and this visit improved relations with Father Sorin for a time. Father Sorin knew of the intrigues being stirred up in Paris and Rome, but he did not take the lead in promoting them. His one concern was to advance the work of Holy Cross in America, and he believed that this required administrative and financial control centered in himself. When that involved siding with Fathers Drouelle and Champeau against his superior general, he did so. But he did it reluctantly.

Father Drouelle in Rome and Father Champeau in Paris were both constantly beset by financial difficulties, just like everyone else. Circumstances were compelling Holy Cross to expand rapidly in all directions, so that expenditures always ran ahead of income. Father Moreau had to assume final responsibility for determining how the scant resources should be spent, and this frequently meant turning down a request from a colleague for approval of a project which might in itself be highly desirable.

Actually the efforts to control expenditures were far from successful. When Father Drouelle ran out of money, he would draw a note on the mother house without warning. He knew that Father Moreau would protest, but he also knew that he would find some way to honor the note. They all thought they were much smarter businessmen than Father Moreau, especially after the experience in 1855 when he had been warning them of an approaching doom that failed to materialize. That long drawn-out lawsuit also aggravated the situation. On the one hand Father Moreau was criticized for putting time and money into it. On the other some of his colleagues acted as though he was owner of the property in dispute and consequently able to take care of all their needs.

Such attitudes contained the seeds of grave mistakes, but nobody could foresee the disastrous fruits they were in fact to yield. A Brother Marie Julien, who had won an admirable reputation as general steward of the mother house, was assigned by the general chapter of 1857 as steward of the house in Paris. The chapter also made him an assistant to the superior general, and as such he had power of attorney to transact business with the Society for the Propagation of the Faith, a major source of funds for the Holy Cross missions.

Brother Marie Julien soon began to think of himself as banker for the entire Congregation, a role in which he was encouraged by Fathers Drouelle, Champeau, and Sorin, each of whom found it convenient to have someone on whom they could draw in an emergency without suffering the recriminations that followed when without authorization they issued a draft for presentation to Father Moreau. The brother was very deft at financial juggling, and he soon built up a series of business contacts who helped him to meet notes as they fell due.

Such was the situation in 1859 when preparations were being made for the general chapter to be held the following year. It may have been a factor in encouraging Father Champeau to try to create for himself in Paris an autonomous regime similar to that already existing in the United States, for in November he wrote urging Father Sorin to come to the chapter to join in persuading the superior general "to change his methods, establish a good novitiate, form his subjects, and imitate the prudence and kindliness of other congregations in his administration, especially his financial administration."

The charges are noteworthy, and they will be repeated over and over without substantial modification or addition until they are believed even by the Holy Father. Yet it is perfectly clear that they are a rationalization on the part of those who formulated them. This is not the true grievance. What they want is to emancipate themselves, to substitute their own will and judgment for that of the superior they had vowed to obey.

Father Sorin prudently decided to stay away from the chapter, but others were drawn into the conspiracy. One of these, a Father Bollard, who had been removed from his post as superior at Rheims because of his poor administration, wrote and distributed a pamphlet which not only declared that under canon law a general chapter's authority was greater than that of a superior general but set out the procedure governing the deposition of a superior general if he was not willing to resign. The Constitutions of Holy Cross did in fact explicitly provide that the authority of the general chapter was superior to that of the superior general.

The impropriety of the pamphlet and its challenge to constituted authority are, nevertheless, too apparent to require amplification.

When he was personally involved, as in this instance, Father Moreau was capable of amazing—perhaps excessive—detachment. He was well aware of the plots, and he knew that only a small minority supported Father Bollard but that it included some of the most prominent members of the Congregation, people he himself had picked for positions of importance. He saw that such insubordination threatened not so much himself as the principle of authority, and he tried to stop it by bringing it into the open. He proposed to the chapter that Father Bollard be deprived of a vote in choosing delegates, pointing out that, since he was no longer a superior, his credentials were not valid. The chapter, however, felt that, though he had stepped out of line, Father Bollard was still entitled to vote, and Father Moreau did not force the issue.

But recriminations soon developed over finances. Complaints were presented that Father Moreau had not kept Holy Cross accounts separate from those of the Good Shepherd convent, which he had continued to direct until 1858, and that he was hiding secret debts which would wreck Holy Cross after his death.

His answer in each case was to cooperate fully with committees appointed to investigate the charges. He repeated his most formal assurances that the only financial transactions in which his administration and he himself were involved were those displayed on the record. He reminded them of his constant efforts to keep everyone informed regarding the financial situation, for example, his circular of January 1, 1857, which listed loans by the mother house to other houses of the Congregation totaling ninety-four thousand francs as the main cause of financial pressure on Sainte-Croix, a pressure that would quickly dissipate if each house repaid its borrowings at the stipulated times. Notre Dame alone had received fifty-five thousand francs in that year.

He reaffirmed that the Sainte-Croix church had not been a burden on the general funds of Holy Cross, for the simple reason that it had inspired additional donations, in proof of which he listed a total of more than a hundred thousand francs contributed expressly for the construction of the mother church.

The investigating committees, having studied the accounts and listened to Father Moreau's explanations, vindicated him completely. It was clear, nevertheless, that confidence had been weakened by this and other incidents before and at the chapter, and he tendered his resignation. This the chapter absolutely refused to accept.

Unfortunately, however, the issues were growing more confused by the day. His enemies continued to accuse him of doing precisely what they themselves were doing, incurring secret debts. And they were suggesting that the real motive for refusing the offered resignation was a fear on the part of the capitulants to assume responsibility for the financial mess which they said Father Moreau had created and must be made to straighten out.

The real financial mess, which would soon explode into a scandal, was brought to the chapter's attention, but it was unwilling to face it. One of the chapter's duties was to examine the accounts of each house of the Congregation. Those for Paris, prepared by Brother Marie Julien, came to them without the countersignature of Father de Marseul, who had been designated to verify them. He had been unable, he said, to get clarification of various items. After trying to avoid a summons, Brother Marie Julien finally appeared before the chapter but refused to explain certain activities on the ground that they were "purely personal."

Instead of insisting on an immediate explanation, the chapter contented itself with Brother Marie Julien's promise that he would make a complete report to his local superior, Father Champeau. The decision was all the more extraordinary, because Father Champeau had already indicated his belief that no explanation was necessary by sponsoring a request to remove Father de Marseul for his refusal to countersign the accounts in the first instance.

The general chapter's casualness on this score contrasts sharply with its detailed examination of the similar charges of deceptive accounting earlier made against the Superior General. It seems intelligible only against the background of what had become, or was rapidly becoming, an organized conspiracy. To present the situation in the family terms which fit in with the original spirit of Father Moreau's plan of organization, the elder children had reached a point at which each felt the urge to take off on his own.

Just as Father Sorin had long been doing in America, other superiors were becoming more concerned with their own local needs than with the overall good of the Congregation. This was particularly true of Father Drouelle in Rome, who was insatiable in his demands for money to build up St. Bridget's, and of Father Champeau in Paris, who was equally dedicated to organizing a center that would, to his way of thinking, make a much better mother house for Holy Cross than the original foundation in Le Mans.

Like Father Sorin, they fought every attempt by the general administration to control their accounts. Father Champeau had been particularly irritated because the Superior General had sent a priest to Paris charged with the duty of tightening up the regime there. This was the same Father de Marseul who refused to certify Brother Marie Julien's accounts as being in order. Forgetting his earlier strictures on Father Sorin, Father Champeau had taken the lead in organizing the opposition, which he described in a letter to Father Sorin as

> a group of older religious organized to bring pres-
> sure to bear on him (the Superior General) by a
> kindly and invincible unanimity. . . . We must make
> use of the right given us by our Rules, and of the cer-
> tain support of the Holy See, in order to become an
> efficient congregation despite ourselves, one worthy

of esteem, able to inspire confidence, and worthy to obtain it.

By the time of the 1860 general chapter, this group had organized to the point where Fathers Drouelle and Champeau could take the leading part in preparing a committee report condemning the Superior General and the general council for having suppressed the vicariates in France, an action they had taken because the functioning of these recently created administrative units had broken down for lack of trained personnel to operate them. After hearing Father Moreau's defense of his action, the general chapter in plenary session rejected the committee report. It, nevertheless, added to the bad impression, and it was undoubtedly a factor in the decision to delegate to Father Champeau the task of clearing up Brother Marie Julien's accounts.

One great satisfaction lightened the sorrows which this chapter showered on Father Moreau. Although Father Sorin had wanted the sisters' chapter to meet at Notre Dame, it was held at Le Mans, and it included delegates from America. The session, as the Annals of the Marianites record, "was calmer than anyone had dared hope," the capitulants agreeing unanimously on most of the serious issues to be decided. They also approved the decrees settling the division of temporal assets between themselves and the priests and brothers, as well as the constitutions to be submitted to Rome, which placed the mother house at Le Mans. The one major point which could not be resolved in Father Sorin's absence was the division of physical assets at Notre Dame, and the matter was again postponed. Finally, and this was for Father Moreau a major consolation, it was decreed that, despite the legal division required by Rome, there would continue "a community of spiritual interests between the sisters and the Congregation of Holy Cross."

After the 1860 general chapter, Father Moreau wrote to the Prefect of Propaganda Fide about some matters of which he was in doubt. The Cardinal's reply, dated September 20, hinted at large-scale irregularities in the conduct of the affairs of Holy Cross. Father Moreau was naturally very upset and asked the Sacred Congregation to clarify. He got little satisfaction, however, partly at least because Father Drouelle as procurator was the go-between and he had no desire to help reveal his own part in these dealings.

His companion in duplicity, the superior in Paris, took an amazing step, which may well have been intended to distract attention from this same problem. In a letter repeating and amplifying the criticisms earlier expressed to Father Sorin, Father Champeau formally denounced his superior general to the Congregation of Propaganda. Father Moreau, he charged, was solely responsible for "the state of suffering" of the congregation. There was no well-organized novitiate in France. The study program was inadequate. There were too many foundations. The financial administration was "incomparably harsh." Though Father Moreau was "a holy man, generous and extremely mortified," he was arbitrary, restless, changeable, a difficult character. He kept everything so much in his own hands that there was no continuity of succession. He could not even be removed because only he knew the resources and workings of the Congregation.

Father Champeau was equally violent in other correspondence, and it is hard not to read into some of his expressions the prickings of a guilty conscience seeking to defend itself. In his letters to Father Drouelle, in particular, he works himself into a frenzy against his Superior General. He pokes fun at prescriptions on observance of the rules, silence, the vow of poverty, stability in the performance of one's obediences. "Have you received the avalanche of circulars being spawned by the press at Sainte-Croix?" he asks. Or, expressing his annoyance at being urged to pay interest on a loan, when the general chapter had extended by a year the time for repayment of the principal, he burst out: "I can stand it no longer. This uncontrolled despotism must cease."

The whispering and insinuations had done their work all too well. Cardinal Barnabo, once Father Moreau's admirer and supporter, had lost confidence in him. In December 1860, he wrote a sharp letter, repeating most of Father Champeau's criticisms, and got back an answer of outraged innocence which did more credit to Father Moreau's honesty than to his diplomacy. Let them, he said, send an apostolic visitor to see for himself and draw his own conclusions.

While the Cardinal was pondering this offer, a committee of three priests sent by Father Moreau to Paris was trying without too much success to unearth the facts about Brother Marie Julien. But a little later, they came to light through another source, and they were worse than the most pessimistic anticipations. Marie Julien, who had thought himself a financier, had been duped by a swindler who had convinced him to invest huge amounts of borrowed money in a bogus stock deal. It was not suggested that Marie Julien wanted the money for his own use. His purpose was to put Holy Cross once and for all on its feet. But the effect was the same.

Father Moreau's investigators and the public authorities were digging simultaneously from different directions. When the storm broke, Brother Marie Julien went into hiding, taking his accounts with him. Creditors began to spring up on all sides. Nobody knew whom to believe. Even Father Champeau was of very little help. He tried to cover up his own major role in creating and permitting the conditions which had made this disaster possible. Rather than face the issues, he began to talk of resigning his position as superior in Paris and even made plans to flee.

Though Father Moreau quickly realized that this blow could be fatal to his work, he kept his head. Concerned only to save the Congregation and its honor, he immediately announced that all notes contracted in the interest of the Paris house would be honored but that he accepted no responsibility for debts incurred by Marie Julien without authority. As for Marie Julien himself, he dispensed him from his vows but told him he could come back at any time after paying off his debts.

A board set up in Paris, with Father Champeau as a member, unanimously agreed that criminal charges should be brought against Marie Julien and the swindlers. The general council at Holy Cross confirmed the findings and directed Father Champeau to sign the complaint.

Father Champeau, however, hesitated to take the decisive step without first checking with the archbishop of Paris, who for his part saw the situation in quite a different light. He wanted no scandal in his archdiocese and said so in most emphatic terms. Holy Cross would have to pay everything and keep the swindle out of the courts and the headlines. Father Moreau protested most strenuously, especially as there was no way to establish the full extent of the obligation he was being asked to assume. But after an interview with the Cardinal, he realized he had no choice.

This was something worse than the darkest forebodings which had crushed him a few years earlier. But a concrete challenge always brought out the best in Father Moreau. He immediately set to work to list the claims, sifted out the many false or exaggerated ones, made deals with those who could be persuaded to wait, and found cash to pay off those threatening quick court action. When all the calculations were made, the total of the verified debts was 235,130 francs. It was an overwhelming debt, equivalent to a quarter of the gross assets of Holy Cross in France.

The two who, apart from Brother Julien, were most to blame, Fathers Drouelle and Champeau, gave absolutely no help. On the contrary, they denounced the investigations as vexatious efforts to embarrass them, and resisted the economies dictated by the need to pay the debts. "How long will you keep up your habit of finding fault with me for every little thing?" Father Drouelle wrote petulantly to his superior, when Father Moreau repeated his prohibition against issuing drafts on the mother house without advance notice. Nothing would seem more obvious as a matter of business practice, to say nothing of the additional obligations imposed by a vow of poverty, yet other superiors were as unwilling as Father Drouelle to accept any share in the austerity needed to pay Marie Julien's debtors. This was one of the defects of running Holy Cross like a family. The children could overspend their allowances and count on their father to work it out some way.

Father Moreau did just that. By superhuman efforts, he paid off or funded seven-eighths of the total in five years, so that by 1866 only thirty-thousand francs remained in short-term obligations. But he got little credit for his heroic and successful struggle. What the dissidents remembered was the hardship, the restriction on programs for expansion, the bitter poverty which all had to share. Complaints continued to pour in to Rome about the tyrannical manner, the authoritarian attitudes, the financial confusion.

If Father Moreau was making greater demands than formerly, his reasons were clear. The Marie Julien affair and the widespread violation of rules and lack of religious spirit it revealed had demonstrated the need to tighten up. The deceits practiced by the colleagues he had chosen as superiors and their poor business sense compelled him to control finances more tightly than ever. On top of this, his personal responsibility terrified him. It was not so much his legal responsibility, except insofar as he had to think of the slur on the religious life and priesthood if he were ever forced to default. His primary concern was that he had always to administer the properties in such a way as to be able to prove in court that they were really his own. One disastrous lawsuit had already shown how ready the courts were to hold that a person in his position was actually a trustee for a forbidden purpose.

For all these reasons, he drew the controls more tightly into his own hands. At the same time, there was much that could not go on the record, lest one day it serve as evidence that in fact Father Moreau's personal affairs and those of Holy Cross were one and the same, thereby subjecting the Congregation to new vexatious attacks of the public authorities. Such vagueness gave substance to the charges that the accounts were confused and that undisclosed obligations existed. But the fault was not Father Moreau's. It was inherent in his situation.

More significant as an indicator of his true attitudes and motivations was the famous circular on devotion to St. Joseph written in February 1861 at the worst of the crisis. This remarkable outpouring of a spiritual mind surveys the origins, the history, and the foundations of Catholic devotion to St. Joseph, "reserved by the mercy of God for the day of trial through which the Church is now passing." It then refers to the financial and other trials of Holy Cross, and asserts that St. Joseph would preserve them if they took him as model in their own lives and spread devotion to him in the world. The impact of this supernatural interpretation of the Congregation's tribulations is heightened by contrast with the self-interested and intemperate language used by some of those who had played a blameworthy part in the Marie Julien disaster.

CHAPTER TWELVE

The Undermining of Authority

F ather Moreau had asked Cardinal Barnabo for an investigation of the charges leveled at his administration, and the Cardinal in August 1861 named Bishop Angebaut of Angers and Bishop Nanquette of Le Mans to conduct it. The former left the matter entirely to his colleague, who started a report but died before completing it. Bishop Angebaut sent the partial report to Cardinal Barnabo and followed with several letters critical of Father Moreau, all based on third-party information.

Bishop Charles Jean Fillion, who succeeded to Le Mans, was a nephew of the Canon Fillion who had been Father Moreau's intimate friend. Father Sorin (a seminary companion of the new bishop) wrote to him on learning of his appointment, suggesting that the superior general's resignation would best solve the crisis of Holy Cross.

The bishop's answer was a model of discretion and sense.

> Would not the abdication of the Father Superior be
> a remedy worse than the ill itself? . . . God has given
> him the qualities most necessary for founders, ardor
> and enthusiastic zeal. . . . It is much more fitting

and honorable for the Congregation to surround its founder with respect and obedience up to the very end, than to hasten by impatient desires the time when he will hand over his power to other hands.

In completing his predecessor's investigation, Bishop Fillion exhibited the same qualities of judgment shown in his reply to Father Sorin. First of all, his report justified the financial management. Debts, including those of Marie Julien and of the Paris house, totaled 344,000 francs, covered three times over by property holdings in excess of a million francs. Income from boarding schools and the brothers' establishments sufficed to meet mortgage payments. What was needed was what Father Moreau had insisted on from the outset: economy, prudence, and scrupulous observance of the rules.

Regarding the moral condition of the Congregation, the bishop said that in the past some subjects had been admitted too easily but that things had improved greatly. The rule was being observed exactly in the professed house and the two novitiates. If the studies left something to be desired, it was because better professors were not obtainable. The defects, in a word, were the defects of all France—too much work, not enough time to prepare clerics, not enough priests to spare for training.

The one criticism leveled specifically at Father Moreau was that he was trying to do too much. He was simultaneously superior general, provincial for France, local superior of the professed house and the secondary school at Le Mans, novice master for brothers and priests, and theology professor. It was wrong, but, in light of what had happened, it was understandable. And not less understandable were the defects of which various people had accused him: an ardent, imperious, and often unduly sharp and changing character. Ardent he always was, but the other elements reflect rather the pressures of the moment than his generous and intensely just nature. As the bishop pointed out, "all of them add that he is filled with faith and love for the Church, and that, even in his excesses, his zeal is always animated with the purest of intentions."

The investigation was thus a vindication of Father Moreau. The only change recommended was that the superior general should unload some of his responsibilities. But the opposition was not converted. In particular, Father Drouelle in Rome continued to play a double game, misrepresenting Father Moreau's actions and reports to the Holy See and misrepresenting its reactions to him. The investigation, which opened so auspiciously for the superior general's critics and promised decisive results, had misfired. However, they did not give up. They would not give up until their founder had been hounded from their midst.

Father Sorin, as his letter to Bishop Fillion indicates, had decided it was time for a new superior general. This reflected neither personal bias against his colleague nor a wish to get the post for himself. The limit of his vision and ambition was America, a broad enough area of activity indeed and one that still shows the fruits of his single-mindedness. He knew that Father Moreau would continue to call on America to help restore economic equilibrium in Europe, would try to restrict expansion in America until this was done, and would try to control his enthusiasms and hunches and protect his colleagues in New Orleans, New York, and Canada from his arbitrariness. A successor installed with his help might give him a freer hand, leaving him in effect superior general of the New World.

Meanwhile, his concern was to protect his own houses from the consequences of the Marie Julien disaster. Admittedly, the approach was a selfish one, but Father Sorin believed there was no hope for France, and the Marie Julien incident merely confirmed his conviction. It would be folly to waste in Europe money and effort critically needed in America. Starting from the premise that the Congregation in France was in effect finished, he felt entitled to operate on his own judgment, ignoring alike appeals for help and directions concerning the government of the American houses.

Other events conspired to enhance his prestige. The endemic French anticlericalism boiled up to such a point that Father Moreau wrote the archbishop of Cincinnati, one of Father Sorin's most stalwart friends, that he feared all members of Holy Cross might be expelled from France and asked if the archbishop would take them in. The letter spoke in glowing terms of Father Sorin, who presumably had suggested the approach, and who presumably was informed by the recipient of the letter's contents. In his reply, the bishop referred to Holy Cross achievements in the United States and promised that a home and a welcome would always exist for the refugees in Ohio.

The American Civil War also raised Father Sorin's stock. His genuine admiration for the United States and its principles combined with his sense of showmanship and timing to make him find ways to participate with the Union forces. Notre Dame priests were among the first to volunteer as chaplains. Notre Dame sisters manned the first field hospitals. General Phil Sherman sent his son to Notre Dame and his daughter to St. Mary's Academy. Meanwhile, sympathies in France because of the historic association with Louisiana were with the South, and so the emotional split widened between Notre Dame on the one hand and the mother house and the New Orleans community on the other.

In 1861 the war was going badly for the North, and panic swept the country. A tremendous credit squeeze developed, bringing such pressure on Notre Dame to pay its extensive debts that the community thought the end had come. Father Sorin rushed back fifty thousand francs raised on a begging tour in Europe to meet the most pressing calls. This was, however, only a drop in the ocean, and even he was at a loss as to where to turn. Then he had an inspiration. With characteristic daring, he started a major building project. He must have plenty of cash, his creditors said to themselves, because nobody is extending new credit now. Not only did they stop pressing for payment, but some of them increased their loans. The crisis was surmounted.

As usual, however, Father Moreau felt the effects of Father Sorin's preoccupations. It was in this same year, 1861, that the Marie Julien scandal broke. In his frantic search for funds, Father Moreau appealed to each house of the Congregation to send whatever it could. They all responded gallantly: Poland, Canada, New Orleans—all but Notre Dame. Only Father Sorin could spare nothing. He was sorry, but he had just started to build. It was the first notification he had given the mother house, notwithstanding repeated promises to get advance approval before incurring extraordinary expenses.

Such episodes strengthened Father Sorin's concept of himself as the man of destiny, convincing him that he should ignore the petty criticisms of the mother house and follow his proven judgment. The protests that followed whenever he violated instructions sent from Sainte-Croix strengthened his belief that a change of administration would be to his advantage. He'd have no interference from Fathers Drouelle and Champeau if they were running things.

Father Drouelle was in fact very helpful to him in Europe during the winter of 1860–61, when he made a personal report to Cardinal Barnabo and the Pope and acheived approval from the Cardinal for two projects, without mentioning that his superior general was opposed to one and only partly informed about the other. His overall idea was unchanged, that the Congregation in America should be cut loose from dependence on France, and Rome's refusal to approve the sisters' constitutions was seized on by him as a means to promote this end.

On his return, he announced that the Constitutions of the Marianites were to be revised, that the Holy Father had given him new authority, and that Father Moreau had named him his assistant with full powers in their regard. He had Bishop Luers of Fort Wayne write that he wanted to establish the mother house of the Marianites at St. Mary's. Father Moreau insisted that the Pope had given him personal and exclusive authority over the sisters until approval of their constitutions and that the mother house must remain at Le Mans. Father Sorin, nevertheless, won a major victory, for Father Moreau authorized him to govern St. Mary's until further notice and promised that the mother general would not exercise her authority over the house.

Disputes soon developed as to the extent of Father Sorin's authority over St. Mary's. He insisted on exercising the powers of a superior general, whereas Father Moreau said he had only delegated ordinary administrative authority, that, for example, sisters might not be admitted to perpetual vows without the approval of the mother general and himself. The documents are inconclusive, though it must be admitted that some of Father Moreau's statements were couched in such broad terms as to make Father Sorin's stand seem reasonable. Thus, in a circular to the sisters dated May 8, 1861, Father Moreau deplored the agitations and dissensions and then said that because of these conditions, he had decided to have Father Sorin "use all his authority, as my representative, to reform these abuses, . . . thus relieving your mother general of all responsibility in this regard until further orders from me."

Bishop Luers gave his undivided support to Father Sorin. "You have been their superior since the beginning of their foundation in this country," he wrote him, "and must continue to be regarded as their founder here." Accordingly, when the general council at Le Mans and Father Moreau sent the superior general's nephew, Father Charles Moreau, to clear up this and other problems, the Bishop forbade him to interfere in the affairs of the sisters.

Father Charles, an apostolic and learned priest, who had been assistant general for ten years, had many qualifications for the assignment. In particular, he was the only fluent English speaker in the general administration. Nevertheless, his choice was unfortunate. He did not understand the Americans, nor they him. He was emotionally too involved in the differences between Father Sorin and his uncle; he regarded the former as an upstart and ingrate. All he could see was that legality was clearly on the side of France; he ignored the dynamics of history and the facts of possession. If he knew the details of his uncle's earlier encounter with Mother Euphrasia Pelletier, he certainly had not learned the lesson.

The result was that he was outwitted at every step. When he tried to convoke a general chapter of the Marianites, Bishop Luers opposed it on the ground that it would be dominated by French sisters, and he got Rome to back him up. Then Bishop Luers obtained authority from Rome to draft the terms of reference for a chapter. When it met in March 1865, it set up one superioress for all American houses with practically unrestricted authority and changed the name from Marianites to Sisters of the Holy Cross. St. Mary's delegates numbered nine of the seventeen capitulants, and the changes were voted by a majority of one.

No doubt Bishop Luers was motivated by a praiseworthy desire to protect the excellent work being performed in his diocese and in the United States by Notre Dame and St. Mary's, but the effect was to convince Cardinal Barnabo that Father Moreau had lost his grip. And this played into the hands of those in Europe seeking to replace him or curb his authority.

While the complicated drama was unfolding in America, the general chapter called for Le Mans in August 1863 opened in an atmosphere of bitterness and recrimination, with the superior general the target of attacks from both sides of the Atlantic and the scapegoat for everyone's mistakes.

Father Moreau was no politician. He knew nothing about building up voting blocs in a deliberative assembly, developing bargaining positions, exploiting differences within the opposition, or protecting oneself against the errors and misjudgments of friends. He relied on truth, honor, and justice, overlooking the fact that humans sometimes fail in their efforts to bring together legality and right.

He was in fact beaten before the chapter began, for the simple reason that the organization of the meeting made him defendant rather than arbiter. Cardinal Barnabo had decided that Bishop Fillion of Le Mans should preside, and Father Moreau welcomed the opportunity for an objective probing of the problems by one who had already proved himself sympathetic. His opponents, however, recognized the implications. At the chapter of the French province, which preceded the general chapter, they attacked and ridiculed the superior general, blaming him for all problems.

Nobody could deny the fact of division and bitterness within the Congregation, and Father Moreau himself was becoming persuaded that his best hope to save his work was to withdraw from its direction. He accordingly offered his resignation when the chapter opened, clearing the way by making a detailed report on recent events, starting with the Marie Julien affair, then setting out the conflicts with Father Sorin, and closing with a review of the state of discipline and religious fervor in the institute.

The chapter had no difficulty in refusing the proffered resignation, though again from mixed motives, some because they wanted no change, others because they thought they could limit the superior general's authority, others again because they feared that the finances were in such a mess that Father Moreau should not be allowed to resign until things were cleared up. The committee investigation of the reports was inconclusive. They agreed in principle with Father Moreau that the superior general represented authority and must be obeyed, but they stopped short of censuring those in America who had flouted that authority.

A discussion of plans to recognize the administrative machinery revealed the extent to which the opposition had gained ground. The committee recommended two provinces, one for Europe and one for America, and Rome added, before approving the decrees, that the provincials should have the widest possible discretion and remain free from interference by the superior general except in cases of grave negligence or real urgency. Yet so far was Father Moreau from regarding the opposition as a clash of individuals that he picked Father Drouelle as vicar to govern the European Province until election of a provincial. Father Drouelle in turn named Father Champeau his assistant, so that the end result of the chapter was to place in key positions two of the men who were determined that they, and not the superior general, should run Holy Cross. Father Sorin continued as superior of Notre Dame, and the provincial chapter of the American houses, held in May 1865, chose him as provincial.

The concessions granted at the 1863 general chapter did nothing to satisfy those opposed to Father Moreau's government. A few months later, Bishop Luers of Fort Wayne sent Cardinal Barnabo a very harsh attack on Father Moreau, written in French, which, combined with its contents, suggests Father Sorin's inspiration. The charges contained nothing new—that the superior general lacked confidence in Notre Dame, that he exercised his authority arbitrarily, that he lacked prudence in handling the many nationalities represented in the community, that the Americans had made every effort to live under him but were reaching the end of their patience.

The Cardinal was impressed, especially when the St. Mary's sisters made similar complaints and recommended the same solution, namely, to give the American houses full liberty of action and protect their savings against claims from Europe.

What followed constitutes one of the least explicable episodes in the entire drama. The Cardinal at first was very hostile, but neither the Holy Father nor he had forgotten the tremendous impression Father Moreau had made on them ever since his first visit to Rome. They had been swayed by his charm, impressed with his holiness, struck by his organizing ability and his magic way of finding people and funds to perform what he undertook. The Cardinal accordingly refused to let Father Moreau persist in the silence he had maintained against all attacks.

Under obedience, Father Moreau answered the accusations one by one. He detailed the sources of the financial problems, showing that the critical debts had been incurred in Paris and Rome without his approval, when Fathers Champeau and Drouelle were superiors of these houses. To the charge of caprice in making appointments, he replied that the chapter filled the top posts by secret ballot and that he appointed to local superiorships and vicariates the very people who now criticized him.

As for the complaints of Bishop Luers of Fort Wayne, he said the underlying motive was the chapter's preference for New York or Philadelphia as seat of the American provincialate over Notre Dame, where Father Sorin "for many years has wanted to move me, along with the mother house."

The entire ground was gone over thoroughly, both in writing and in face-to-face confrontations in the cardinal's office with Father Moreau and his two recalcitrant sons. The outcome was a complete vindication of the former. "Either these men are fools or criminals," the cardinal commented of Fathers Champeau and Drouelle, "or else they are staging some kind of devilish comedy for my benefit." The authenticity of this remark is unquestionable, for it was inserted by Father Moreau in a circular letter addressed to the entire community. It indicates how completely the cardinal was convinced, but it also reveals something of the irascible and violent character of the cardinal, which had already swung from one extreme to the other and back again, and which would once more swing violently against Father Moreau.

For the moment, however, all was peace and light. Pius IX renewed his earlier marks of favor. Three times he received Father Moreau in private audience, amply consoling him for all he had suffered and urging him to greater efforts to see that the Rule was strictly observed. The detail is significant, since a major complaint of his critics was that he was always pushing them too hard.

The Pope's overriding concern, as is understandable, was not to fix responsibility for the past but to make a settlement which would permit this important Congregation to concentrate on the mission for which it had been founded. He accordingly insisted on a reconciliation and received Fathers Drouelle and Champeau with their superior in special audience. It was agreed that Father Drouelle would not be reinstated as procurator in Rome (as he wanted) but would be kept in office as provincial of France.

After the two left Rome, Cardinal Barnabo went into the situation in America with the same thoroughness, and with the same result. Father Moreau's explanations convinced him completely. A memorandum of Father Sorin criticizing Father Charles Moreau's frustrated investigation incensed him particularly against its author. "It is high time," he said, "that people learn to have more respect for authority, because otherwise those people will have to be put out."

Father Moreau, as is abundantly clear in particular from the circular letter of January 31, 1864, which reports in detail to the Congregation on the reason for his visit to Rome and its results, was overwhelmingly gratified by the renewal of the Holy See's confidence in him. He was, nevertheless, equally concerned by the definite proofs that three outstanding subjects, his top lieutenants, had been conspiring against him over a long period. Convinced that the compromise solution proposed by Rome would not work, he twice asked the cardinal to let him resign so that Holy Cross could make a new start under a new head. It was only when Pius added his personal refusal to that of Cardinal Barnabo that he bowed to duty.

The sincerity and dedication with which he did his part are recorded in the circular letters and other communications he sent to the members of Holy Cross during the following critical months. While the administrative reforms and other measures ordered by the 1863 general chapter could not take effect until approved by the Holy See, he began immediately to attack the problems revealed by the chapter and by the subsequent discussions in Rome.

His first concern was for the religious formation of subjects, stressing the top priority of properly constituted novitiates for both priests and brothers directed by highly qualified novice directors. Next, he developed the importance of respect for authority, while setting out the procedures to permit expression of legitimate complaints. Then he detailed prescriptions to combat abuses: prohibition of the ill-fated drafts which had caused

Marie Julien's downfall, definition of rules to determine how much each house should contribute toward paying the Marie Julien debts, prompt return of statistics and budgets, injunction of building or other extraordinary spending without approval.

Simultaneously, Father Moreau engaged in two further major projects, the drafting of a general plan of studies for use in all schools and a revision of the rules prescribed by the 1863 chapter. The latter task he completed in June 1864, even though (as he notes in the letter of transmission) he had to do all the work himself because none of his assistants would undertake it. Such a detail is a significant comment on his techniques as superior. He himself did the job rather than force an unwilling subject. Also significant is another remark in the same letter. I worked hard on this revision, he said, but it is not by any means perfect, and I want the next chapter to go over it point by point and weigh every objection. There is nothing arbitrary or dictatorial in that approach.

He could not finish the plan of studies because information on current teaching practices in some schools had not arrived. The circular letter repeating his request for the material contains a charming note which shows that the pressures had not routed his sense of humor. He had heard, he wrote, that corporal punishment was still practiced in some schools, and this reminded him of the abbot who complained to St. Anselm that, though they continually whipped their students, they only grew worse. "And when they grow up, how are they?" the saint asked. "Stupid as beasts," replied the abbot.

It was not till November 1864 that the decrees of the previous year's general chapter were released by Cardinal Barnabo's office, and the text as approved confirmed Father Moreau's worst premonitions. Something mysterious had indeed occurred after he left Rome. While he was rebuilding the Congregation and restoring confidence and union, his opponents had been busy undermining him. They had persuaded the Cardinal to alter key provisions. Paris was designated as the seat of the French province, and Notre Dame as that of America. The sisters in America were placed under the jurisdiction of Bishop Luers of Fort Wayne, and the priests and brothers under the immediate supervision of the same bishop, while the superior general was instructed to leave administrative details to his subordinates and to intervene only in cases of grave negligence or real urgency.

The principle was a legitimate one, but its formulation at that moment and in that context was a proclamation of his opponents' victory. The mother house would exercise no further authority in the New World. Bishop Luers and Father Sorin would see to that. And even in Europe, the dissidents could do pretty much as they liked.

What had happened since the general chapter was that the opposition had reformed and resumed its intrigues. Notre Dame, specifically, had engaged in a power squeeze. Father Sorin suppressed the foundation in Philadelphia and closed six schools with a combined enrollment of twelve hundred children, in order to eliminate this logical location for the provincial house. How unjustified this action was can be inferred from the reaction of an impartial witness, the superior of the Augustinians in Philadelphia and a member of the bishop's council. "In all my knowledge of the history of religious orders, and of the acts of superiors of religious societies," he wrote at the time, "I have never heard or known of anything equal to the insane and reckless conduct of the authorities of South Bend in shutting up the houses of your society here."

Also under Father Sorin's inspiration, and in pursuance of the same objectives, Bishop Luers had gone to Rome and persuaded Cardinal Barnabo that the broadest discretionary authority should be given to himself in the affairs not only of the sisters but also of the priests and brothers. The results were seen in the acts of the provincial chapter of the priests and brothers held at Notre Dame in 1865. It made Notre Dame supreme over all the other American houses, and it achieved an effective total autonomy of America vis-à-vis France. Henceforth, insistence on its rights by Le Mans could lead only to an open break. As Bishop Fillion expressed the situation the following year to Cardinal Barnabo, "The separation (of America from the mother house) is already carried out in their hearts."

In order to get Cardinal Barnabo to give him discretionary powers over Holy Cross in America, Bishop Luers had had to reawaken His Eminence's doubts regarding Father Moreau's administrative and financial ability, but that was not too difficult, because the Cardinal was unfortunately a man who tended to be swayed by the latest impression. In this context, Father Moreau's exhortations to a more exact observance of the rule were interpreted as improper interference in the routine operation of the houses, his insistence on common responsibility for Marie Julien's debts, an attempt to evade the personal obligation he had assumed under pressure from the Archbishop of Paris.

It is on this relatively secondary point that the supreme crisis developed. A major element in the rapid growth of Holy Cross had been Father Moreau's ability to raise the money needed to build so many houses, to send missionaries across the world and support them in inhospitable places, to operate vast works of charity and education. Much of the capital had been given to him personally by people who recognized his uprightness, holiness, and zeal. More had been placed in his name because of the French laws forbidding gifts for religious purposes. All of it he had handled so well that he could command extensive credit on no greater security than his word and signature. His public status was such that he had weathered the onset of the Marie Julien debts, and each year he was cutting down the balance substantially.

But this meant an intensification of austerity all round, and the superior general's principal aides were not prepared to match him in sacrifice. Certainly none of them shared his magnificent sense of justice. While the determinant of his action was that money had been borrowed and had to be repaid, they, in different ways and for different reasons, were willing to take advantage of the creditors of Holy Cross. And so the proposal, long ago whispered, was now being peddled openly. Let the mother house be sold, let Father Moreau go bankrupt, but we must save what we can of our other assets.

Father Sorin was clear. America would hold what it had. Father Drouelle in Paris was equally clear. He used all his influence to prevent the implementation of a decision of the 1863 general chapter, a decision in which Bishop Fillion had concurred. The chapter had decided that the Paris house should be abandoned when the lease expired, since it saw no way to raise the two hundred thousand francs which would be needed to buy and equip a new building. He finally persuaded Father Moreau to allow him to undertake the effort of saving the foundation on his own responsibility, establishing a separate civil society in which Father Champeau and he became shareholders, and endowing it with considerable assets of the existing Paris house. The transfer of assets was carried out in violation of his agreement with the Superior General and his council, and it would later become a source of additional misunderstandings and differences.

Father Drouelle also succeeded in achieving a major gain as a result of an action intended to curb his powers. The provincial chapter held in August 1864 decided that the provincial house should be moved from Paris to Le Mans. By clever maneuvering, however, he was able to persuade Bishop Fillion that the action represented an insult to him, because the general chapter of the previous year, over which he had presided as apostolic delegate, had designated Paris, and the provincial chapter had failed to consult him before reversing that decision. The effect was very serious for Father Moreau, who was represented as the one really responsible for the provincial chapter's offense, for it affected the bishop's overall view of him.

Father Drouelle was also able to utilize the incident to influence Cardinal Barnabo, on whom constant pressure was maintained until he finally decided to summon Father Moreau once more to Rome to see if he could persuade him to go along with what seemed to be the common view of the leading members of the Congregation.

The Cardinal's position was not a happy one. He had no personal squabble with the superior general. But his job was to protect the major asset which the Congregation of Holy Cross represented for the Church. And if (as so many alleged) the superior general was losing his grip, was allowing himself to be influenced by unreasonable scruples, was threatening the very life of Holy Cross by his obstinacy, he had to seek a compromise.

For Father Moreau, there could be no compromise. Justice was at stake, and so was the principle of authority. Even to leave Le Mans was already to default in his obligations to his creditors. Rumors were rife that he was about to abscond, and, if he left, some might foreclose and ruin all possibility of gradually repaying everything. In his absence, further assets might be removed surreptitiously to defraud the creditors. He accordingly told the Cardinal that he would accept any and all decisions without question, but he could not come. The Cardinal, however, continued to insist, and he finally yielded and set out in January 1866.

In his heart he now knew that the situation was hopeless. Yet he never wavered in his faith and generosity. On the one hand, he felt it his duty to insist on the sacredness of his obligations in justice and the need to maintain the principle of authority within the Congregation. On the other, he strove to avoid allowing any personal feelings on his part to increase the peril to his work.

Once more, at the insistence of the Pope himself, he went over all the old ground, established his own financial responsibility and solvency, demonstrated to the Cardinal's satisfaction the falsity of the accusations. Then he offered his solution. To establish the principle of authority, those responsible for the crisis should be reprimanded, and Father Drouelle should be demoted. But feelings had reached a point where he was no longer acceptable to all, and accordingly he added that he would resign and work under a new superior general to restore concord and confidence. He was, he said, ready to turn over all property in his name, including his own, to a new administration, provided only that he was relieved of financial responsibility.

The objectivity of the analysis and the impartiality of the conclusions almost make one wonder if this man, now in his late sixties, still retained any of our human frailties or emotions. It is only the testimony of others that gives us an inkling of the depths of physical and mental suffering that coexisted within him. For five years, ever since the Marie Julien scandal broke, he had not had a moment's repose—especially for the past two, since the last general chapter, the pressures had been intolerable. They thought he was at the brink of death when he arrived back at Le Mans on June 10, 1866, "haggard with fatigue and black with dust." The doctor recorded in his report a condition of general weakness, loss of weight, and change in features caused by worry, insomnia, and malnutrition. In addition, he was suffering from bronchitis, dyspepsia, and incipient disease of the optic nerve, calling for prolonged treatment and absolute rest.

There were thus legitimate reasons for releasing him from the burdens of office, and that is what Cardinal Barnabo did shortly after his return. But there were none for the harsh personal letter the Cardinal wrote, directing him to refrain from scheming and interference, for his only interference was to continue to insist that until he was relieved of financial responsibility, justice bound him to protect the rights of creditors in the properties still in his name. Obviously, the Cardinal had again listened to other voices after he left.

Yet not even this injustice could deflect Father Moreau from the main issue. Expressing the calm and happiness he undoubtedly felt, he immediately handed over authority to the one designated by the Cardinal to act as vicar-general until an election could be held. This was neither Father Sorin nor Father Champeau. Cardinal Barnabo and Bishop Fillion had discussed several candidates, and they had come to the conclusion that the most prudent choice would be Father Chappé. "He is not a man of brilliant talents," was the way the bishop summed him up, and he has neither the prestige of learning nor that of eloquence. But he is a true religious who seeks only the glory of God, and he has always sided with his superior in past discussions, without losing the esteem and affection of the opposition.

Immediately on being notified of the appointment of a successor, Father Moreau took all steps in his power for the smooth transfer of authority. On June 21, 1866, he himself carried his few belongings from the superior general's room to the room Father Chappé had assigned him. He wrote a last circular announcing to the Congregation the Holy See's decisions, and he had it read to the community in the chapter room after night prayers. After promising "exemplary obedience to the superior general canonically elected," he declared: "I can only thank God for this news. . . . Count always on my devotedness to the Congregation."

That Father Moreau's protestations were not verbal only but were backed by his actions was confirmed by his successor a few days later, when he reported to the Congregation of Propaganda that, far from being in the way, Father Moreau "is helping me by a humility and an obedience which make all of us ashamed of ourselves." Such would be his attitude to the end.

CHAPTER THIRTEEN

The Supreme Sacrifice

To hand over authority was easy for Father Moreau, but to disengage himself from the personal obligations assumed over the years in the interest of Holy Cross was as complicated as was the network of intricate devices by which he had maintained the Congregation's precarious existence.

An imprudent move by Father Drouelle demonstrated the delicacy of the balance. One of his contentions had been that selling some properties would improve the financial position, and he decided to start with Maulévrier, a chateau in the diocese of Angers which had been donated to Father Moreau in 1855 and accepted for use as a boarding school and novitiate. But when he put it on the market, the courts ruled that his action proved the property to have been illegally donated to Holy Cross, though in Father Moreau's name. An important asset thus disappeared without any corresponding reduction in the debts.

In the old days, Father Moreau would have thought of something. He always did. But he was no longer allowed to help. Much of the property was in his name, and he was personally committed—both legally and morally—as guarantor of all debts. Yet the new administration was determined to ignore him, and it had gotten Cardinal Barnabo to warn him to stay on the sidelines. This he did faithfully, except when his conscience forced him to defend the rights of a creditor, but he could not help grieving as he watched the plans develop to dismember the mother house.

The loss of Maulévrier confirmed Father Drouelle's conviction that the solution was to sell Sainte-Croix; and to lay the groundwork, his supporters had Father Moreau excluded from the general chapter called in 1866 to elect a new superior general. He did not protest the exclusion, but he insisted on submitting a report on his administration, in which he reaffirmed the obligation in justice to recognize and protect the rights of those who had aided Holy Cross with loans or credits.

The chapter left the fate of the mother house undecided. Its members sincerely wanted to save the Congregation and heal the internal divisions, and they picked a superior acceptable to all parties. This was Bishop Pierre Dufal, who as apostolic vicar in Bengal was physically and emotionally remote from the embroilment.

The remoteness, however, had disadvantages. There was a long delay before Bishop Dufal reached France, an interval during which the financial situation grew steadily worse, and when he came, he had to go over a lot of old ground to learn the facts for himself.

Father Moreau once more submitted memoranda presenting his version of events, but no longer with any hope except to keep the record straight. The decisions made by Rome could not be reversed. He did, nevertheless, achieve one major objective almost immediately. Bishop Dufal recognized his right to be freed of personal obligation for debts incurred or guaranteed by him on behalf of other members of the Congregation. The bishop accordingly went into the complicated accounts and gave him the releases he had been requesting for years.

Bishop Dufal was impressed by the humility and detachment of the man he had long known and revered. What he saw did not fit in with the reasons presented to him by the new administration for forcing the superior general out of office. But the more he tried to reconstruct the events of the power struggle within the Congregation which had led to his own appointment as superior general, the more confused and perplexed he became. Even the part played by Rome failed to make sense. For example, just a couple of months after acceptance of Father Moreau's resignation, the Holy See in February 1867 approved the Constitutions of the Marianite Sisters for a trial period of two years, confirming the ideas of Father Moreau on a variety of disputed points, keeping the mother house at Le Mans and retaining Father Moreau as superior general. Nor was this a question of one administrative body not knowing what another was doing. The decision came from Cardinal Barnabo's own Congregation of Propaganda, and over his signature.

In his perplexity, Bishop Dufal went to Rome for guidance. His reception by Pius IX in a ninety-minute audience brought out several significant points. It highlighted the Pope's recognition of the importance to the Church of the institution built in thirty years by Father Moreau. Notwithstanding all the conflicts, the facts were impressive. The Congregation numbered five hundred religious distributed in nearly a hundred houses in France, Algeria, Canada, the United States, and Bengal. Their colleges and schools were educating no less than eleven thousand children and youth.

On the other hand, the audience proved that the Pope was convinced that the differences between the founder and his opponents were too deep-seated for compromise and that as a practical matter Bishop Dufal would have to work with the new administration rather than lean on Father Moreau. This did not mean that the new group had the Holy See's full confidence. There were many evidences to the contrary. For example, Bishop Dufal had brought Father Drouelle with him to answer in person charges made against him by reputable persons. His presence was pointedly ignored both by Cardinal Barnabo and by the Pope, and he finally left without seeing anyone.

One other important point impressed on Bishop Dufal in Rome was that the Holy See would not make his decisions for him. His colleagues and he had to develop their own solutions. And when he surveyed the possibilities in the light of this knowledge, he reached the conclusion that the task was beyond his powers. In a formal report to Cardinal Barnabo, he claimed that he had been tricked into accepting the post of superior general by a misrepresentation of the facts. He had been led to believe that the internal crisis could be resolved by dismissing the principal fomenters of disorder (Father Moreau's backers) and that economic solvency could be restored by selling the house in Rome or by floating a loan. Neither was the case, and accordingly he asked the Cardinal to regard his acceptance of the post as having never been given.

When the general council in France learned, as it did from Bishop Dufal himself, what he had done, there was consternation. A prolonged discussion, nevertheless, produced no more constructive proposals than a recommendation to Cardinal Barnabo to remove Father Moreau from the mother house and free him of all obligations as a religious, retain Bishop Dufal as superior general at least until election of a successor, and dispense from their vows any who might so request.

A simultaneous direct appeal to Bishop Dufal not only failed to change his decision but brought a stinging reply expressing his outrage at the way they had deceived him, accusing Father Chappé and his colleagues of responsibility for the evils they had piled up for Holy Cross and reaffirming that he would not become the executor of their plans. Specifically, as he wrote Father Moreau about the same time, that he had no intention of carrying out their proposal "to chase you away" from the mother house.

Cardinal Barnabo's reaction was that it was impossible to get the members of Holy Cross together on any basis, and he began to talk seriously of dissolving the Congregation. Father Drouelle, nevertheless, refused to give in. The same obstinacy of character with which he had led the fight against the founder now served to keep Holy Cross from falling over the precipice, to the edge of which he had pushed it. He bombarded Cardinal Barnabo with a series of proposals, each of which the Cardinal rejected as crazy, but all of which had the cumulative effect of postponing a decision and finally winning him round to agreeing to one more experiment.

The final experiment, as assembled from Father Drouelle's brainstorms, was to be a general chapter in Rome "to decide life or death," with the Cardinal as moderator. It would restore financial solvency by repudiating obligations toward the Marianites, disengaging some French houses, and letting the deeply mortgaged ones sink. Father Moreau would be invited so that Cardinal Barnabo could finally destroy his influence. And Father Sorin would be elected superior general.

Whatever reservations one may have, the program was realistic. Father Sorin was particularly logical for superior general. He already controlled Holy Cross in America, where his reputation was high with both the hierarchy and the public; and while he had kept discretely in the background in the final dispute with Father Moreau, he was friendly with the members of the new administration and shared their views on the need to retrench in France. Even more important, he alone had resources and credit. His election would restore confidence, and he might even share some of his wealth with his needy brethren in Europe.

From the time his resignation had been accepted two years earlier, Father Moreau had honorably abstained from interference in the general administration of Holy Cross. He continued to live at Le Mans, quickly developing for himself a way of life as busy as that he had always led. He took up his residence at the Solitude of St. Joseph, at a little distance from the mother house. And as always, when his duties permitted, the call to the interior life asserted itself. He devoted long hours to meditation, to the attentive recitation of the Office, and to his favorite spiritual readings. Among the books which he treasured and recommended were *The Practice of Christian Perfection, The Knowledge and*

Love of Jesus Christ, The Ascetical Directory, and *The Spiritual Combat*. He also thought very highly of St. Alphonsus Liguori's *Treatise on the Religious Vocation* and *Visits to the Blessed Sacrament*, Bossuet's *Discourse on Universal History*, Fenelon's *Conversations on Prayer*, and de Ligny's *Life of Christ*.

Simultaneously, he increased his correspondence with the Marianite Sisters in France, Canada, and New Orleans, devoting equal attention to their spiritual progress and to the administrative problems, which as their superior general he was asked to solve.

Nor did this activity, though coupled with the already mentioned reports prepared for the general chapter of 1866 and for Bishop Dufal, exhaust his energies. He had never, even in the most trying moments of his administration, ceased to give missions and retreats, and he now at the age of sixty-eight he flung himself once more into this work with all the enthusiasm of a young man. He preached a three-week mission at Grand-Luce in the fall of 1866 and a twelve-day retreat at Flers during the Lent of 1867. The mission at Coulombiers in March 1867 was so successful that pastors of two neighboring parishes had to be called in to help with confessions.

The daily timetable in these missions was most strenuous. Father Moreau preached to the women at 6:30 in the morning, to the men at 8:15, to the whole parish at 10:30, to the women again at 2 p.m. and the men at 4, and finally to everyone at 6:30. "They tell me I look tired," he wrote his sister the last day of the Coulombiers mission, "but, unless I lose my voice, I shall begin another mission this evening." That was at Saint-Christophe, and from there he returned to Flers, and then to yet another mission at Chateau-du-Loir.

Such was his routine, and it was while preaching a mission at Grand-Luce in 1868 that he received a list of the religious chosen to decide "the life or death" of the Congregation at the extraordinary general chapter to be held in Rome. These had been handpicked by Father Drouelle, and he immediately decided that his presence would only create the impression that he had concurred in decisions in conflict with his most cherished ideals.

Another reason soon developed to strengthen his determination to stay in Le Mans. The local newspaper reported in June that the Jesuits had bought the institution formerly directed by Father Moreau. The news threw the religious living in the mother house into dismay, and their superior cabled Bishop Dufal in Rome for a denial. No denial was forthcoming, for, while the report was premature, negotiations were in progress. Under the circumstances, in order to protect the good name of Holy Cross and reassure the creditors, Father Moreau published a newspaper denial, saying the sale could not take place without the unanimous agreement of the civil society which owned the college and that he as a member would not consent. He was convinced that his departure from Le Mans would be taken as a confirmation of current rumors and further jeopardize the situation of the mother house.

He accordingly was not present when the chapter opened on July 14. Some weeks earlier, he had been notified by telegram that the Pope had ordered him to attend. To this telegram he replied immediately with a petition to the Pope explaining his reasons for not going and undertaking to abide by whatever decisions might be taken. He also explained his stand fully to his spiritual director, Father Paulinus, a monk of La Trappe, and was assured by him that his conduct was blameless.

The chapter took only a week for its business, devoting most of the time to a one-sided and undocumented review of the events of the previous several years, and concluding that Father Moreau was responsible for all the Congregation's troubles. It decreed that the mother house must be sold and ended its sessions by electing Father Sorin superior general.

Not only the decisions but a long and bitter attack on Father Moreau, presented in terms which seemed to question his honesty, were incorporated in a circular sent immediately both to the religious of Holy Cross and to the general public. It reached

Le Mans and was read to Father Moreau on August 1. The same day, he received word from Rome that his reasons for refusing to go there were disallowed and that he should make known within four days, under penalty of suspension, if he was now prepared to go.

He did not have to hesitate before answering, for submission not only to the commands but to the wishes of the Holy See were always a characteristic of his attitudes and behavior. Two years earlier he had written Cardinal Barnabo that his greatest trial had been to see himself calumniated at Rome and thus exposed to losing the good will of the Holy See, "to which I have consecrated the whole of my priestly life, teaching what it teaches, and endeavoring to induce others to conform to its prescriptions without any exception." Since it was clear to him that the Pope knew all the facts and still insisted that he should go to Rome, his only choice was to obey. He replied, accordingly, that he would leave just as soon as he could take certain steps made necessary by "the libelous letter" published against him by the general chapter. His first decision had been to accept the humiliations and remain silent, but the organized publicity given the letter convinced him that silence would cause scandal, especially as he was pictured as "in open revolt against the Holy See." Without a moment's delay he prepared his reply in which he presented a detailed and documented account of all his major financial and administrative transactions, backed up by long extracts from minutes of the general chapters which had approved them.

As soon as this was done, despite the intense heat of the season, he set out for Rome and arrived on August 15. Apparently the main reason for insisting that he should come was to convince him that no alternative existed to the sale of the mother house, as decreed by the general chapter.

The diplomatic proprieties were fully observed both by Cardinal Barnabo and by the Pope, when they in turn received him in audience. The Holy Father was effusive in his manner. He readily accepted a letter setting out "the secret workings of the intrigue" of which Father Moreau had been victim. Cardinal Barnabo encouraged him to draw up a new report. But the decisions had been taken. The Pope absolutely vetoed a proposal of Father Moreau to gather round him in some house the religious who had remained loyal to the old Holy Cross. His work as a leader was at an end. In his retirement, he was told, he was free either to leave Notre Dame de Sainte-Croix or stay there "in that part which will not be sold." That was all that was settled when he left Rome on September 3 to return to Le Mans.

It now remained only to work out the details, but even the details could be very bitter. Father Moreau no longer hoped to prevent the liquidation of the mother house, with all it represented for himself and for the Congregation, but he could and did still strive to perform the last rites with honor. His sense of justice compelled him to insist that the creditors who had stood by Holy Cross had first claim on all assets. They had relied on his word, and he would not let them down.

Many of the creditors of Holy Cross held unsecured notes accepted in the first instance, not with any desire to make a profit but simply to help Father Moreau when as superior general he was pressed for money. They included his sisters, brothers-in-law, and nephews, all poor people who could ill afford the loss of the amounts they had generously advanced in emergencies. The new administration, however, judged it proper to explore legal loopholes, even though it meant depriving these creditors of their rights. The measures they adopted included removal of furniture and sale of cattle from the property, thereby reducing the value of the assets, as well as raising a new secured loan of seventy-five thousand francs, which automatically took legal precedence over the unsecured creditors.

It was more than Father Moreau could stand. When he realized what was taking place, he decided as a member of the civil society in which legal ownership was vested to move in the courts for its liquidation and thus protect the creditors.

The request, filed before the civil tribunal of Le Mans on November 19, 1868, asked for the appointment of a court administrator, with power to convert the assets of the civil society into cash without recourse to the courts. Uncanonical loans and considerable debts had been added, it said, so that the society found itself burdened with new liabilities which "it had not contracted, which were of a harmful nature, and of which it was unable to explain either the causes or the origin."

His move was denounced as treachery and malice, and Father Sorin countered by ordering him under obedience to desist. Father Moreau realized the seriousness of his stand, but he had fully weighed the pros and cons, and he was convinced that the demands of natural justice dictated this course.

> I owe it to those persons who have honored me with their confidence, and who have lent me money either with or without collateral, to take action on their behalf. That is why I am today bound to reach an understanding with these people either directly or through my representative, in order to secure for them the best possible settlement for the property which I entrusted to the civil society, without keeping any part of what belongs to me personally, should this prove necessary. What I want above all, insofar as lies in my power, is to avoid loss to any person who lent me money while I was superior.

His conscience was, accordingly, clear. "Not even legitimate superiors," he wrote to the bishop who had sided with Father Sorin, "can command in virtue of the vow of religion except insofar as their orders inflict no grave harm on truth, justice, and charity."

In such an atmosphere of recriminations and public bitterness, with legal maneuvers and counter maneuvers, a constable arrived one day in February 1869 with a writ of attachment. The document listed the property of Sainte-Croix in the Street of

Notre Dame, the building with the square-tiled roof, the court-yard planted with lemon trees, and all the adjoining land, pieces of land, and gardens. Also included were the Solitude of the Savior and the Solitude of St. Joseph.

The writ of attachment had been secured through a move of the new administration intended to eliminate Father Moreau from the picture and thwart his plans to guard all the assets for the creditors. His application to the courts was to initiate a voluntary liquidation under court supervision, to be conducted at a leisurely pace and permit realization of the full value of the assets. This was the more important because the buildings were of so specialized a nature as to be valuable only for purposes similar to those for which they were constructed. It might be necessary to wait a long time to find a buyer prepared to pay a price related to their intrinsic worth.

The writ of attachment, however, changed the situation from one of voluntary liquidation to one of forced liquidation in bankruptcy, and, as preparations began under its provisions for auctioning off first the contents and then the property itself, Father Moreau had to decide what he should do. Despite pressures to withdraw from Le Mans, he decided to remain on the spot to enlighten the liquidators on whatever can increase the assets and cut down the liabilities of our civil society, in order that the interests involved be not harmed by a false picture of the financial situation.

He moved across the street to a small house occupied by his two sisters, where he installed himself in a tiny room, a little more than nine feet long and seven wide. It was ample for his few belongings. He had brought with him a bed that had formerly belonged to his venerated friend, Canon Louis Jean Fillion. This he could remove as a "necessity," though in fact he did not use a bed. For twenty years he had slept in an armchair, which he had to buy at the officially determined price of 52.50 francs before he was allowed to remove it. He did not possess even that trifling sum, and the Mother General of the Marianites had to find it. The rest of his belongings were carried by Father Charles and himself in their arms. They were a few items of clothing, some books valued at six francs, his ordination certificates, and about a thousand copies of the hymns which he used when preaching missions and retreats.

Squabbles, negotiations, deals, and auctions continued for many months before Sainte-Croix was emptied of all its possessions and its affairs wound up. The buildings designed to serve as high school and community residence were bought through an intermediary by the Bishop of Le Mans, who planned to install a community of Jesuits and reopen the school. Father Moreau made no effort to interfere. Rather, he was happy to know that there was now a good likelihood that the educational work he had begun at Sainte-Croix would be carried on by the sons of St. Ignatius for whom he had the greatest affection and respect. His concern remained what it had been during the entire episode, namely, to ensure that the creditors were repaid what they had lent to the Congregation of Holy Cross. The obligation was one of justice, he continued to insist, and not only Sainte-Croix but all the property of the Congregation was morally obligated. Although he wrote to the liquidators about this time in these terms, his pleadings continued to be ignored.

In the struggle and confusion, many things were neglected. The rights of the Marianite Sisters, for example, had been specifically defined by the Congregation of Propaganda, which had instructed Father Sorin to provide another house for them if Sainte-Croix were sold. But nothing was done about it, and they moved the administration to a house near the one occupied by Father Moreau and his sisters.

Neither was provision made for Father Moreau's future. Apparently the subject was raised by someone, for a note by a member of the general administration exists to the effect that it was decided that Holy Cross could offer him nothing. However, his needs were slight, and they were met by the Marianites who each day brought food to him and his sisters.

What concerned him more than his material future was his canonical status. The Pope had specifically told him that he was free to pick whatever place he wanted to live, and the Congregation of Propaganda had denied several requests during previous years to send him to a house away from Le Mans. He was, nevertheless, worried about the obligations of his vow of poverty, and he asked Monsignor Simeoni, secretary to the Congregation of Propaganda, for authorization to follow the advice of his confessor. The monsignor sent the letter to Father Sorin, who offered a radical solution typical of his approach to problems. He asked Propaganda to dispense Father Moreau entirely from his vows. Propaganda for its part was not used to dealing so casually with founders of religious congregations. As at all times, it paid Father Moreau the courtesy of asking him if that was what he wanted. His answer left the matter undecided, and so it remained.

He was in his seventieth year when he left Sainte-Croix. Few of his contemporaries were still alive, and even fewer physically and mentally active. Yet, despite recent cruel experiences, despite a lifetime of intense work and a rigid personal regime, it never occurred to him for a moment to slow down.

He continued his assiduous attention to the affairs of the Marianites, whose superior general he still was, exhorting, encouraging, and directing both by word of mouth and by letter. Thanks to the determination of Bishop Luers, who wanted no French interference in his diocese, the sisters at Notre Dame had set up a separate administration under the title of Sisters of the Holy Cross. All the others, however, in Canada and New Orleans as well as in France had joyfully accepted the Constitutions as approved by the Congregation of Propaganda in 1867.

Much of Father Moreau's copious correspondence both with superiors and with individual sisters has been preserved. To read it is to be impressed by the clarity and precision of his mind, the grasp alike of detail and of broad implication, the intense concern for the welfare of each individual and for the work to which they were dedicated.

These letters also picture how he felt and thought. "I am not yet dying," he wrote the superioress at New Orleans in November 1871, and I still hope to be able to preach this Lent in a parish in our diocese, notwithstanding my 72 years. Just the same, old age is warning me that I am drawing near the end, and I am anxious to see God and to be able not to offend Him any more.

As the letter indicates, he was still giving missions and other spiritual exercises. A note book in the archives of the Marianites records work in fifty parishes in the five years following his resignation as superior general of Holy Cross at the end of 1866. Missions, retreats, Ways of the Cross, Forty Hours, Lenten series, the Month of Mary, he was available for every kind of preaching engagement. Most of his work was in rural areas, but he also visited large villages and small cities.

The people loved the aged preacher. They saw him appear in the pulpit, a little stooped, his head inclined slightly on the right shoulder, and his features breathing an air of austerity blended with kindness. As he left the church, he stopped to chat with the people and was full of that kind consideration that gave him the air of a saint.

When home at Le Mans, he said his daily Mass in the chapel of the Marianites, and he returned there in the afternoon to visit the Blessed Sacrament, recite his Breviary, and make the Way of the Cross. In the evening he read to the sisters from *The Lives of the Saints*, commenting informally on the text. Afterward he said the rosary with them and closed with night prayers.

With all of this, he found time for a task he considered of great importance, the correction and revision of a book of meditations he had first published in 1848. The new edition modified the original plan in order to link up the meditations with the liturgical cycle. Into this work went the spiritual wisdom distilled from his own long trial and humiliation. He knew his days were numbered, and he wanted to continue his apostolate beyond the limits of his lifetime.

> May these meditations, undertaken solely for the
> glory of God and the sanctification of souls, continue
> to make religion known and loved when I shall no
> longer be able to write, speak, or act.

These were the closing words of the book issued in September 1872.

He still continued his lifelong regime of extreme abstemiousness. He ate only one full meal a day, with a light collation in the evening. He drank nothing but water, and he fasted three days a week. Nevertheless, his health remained generally very good. Only his eyesight, which had begun to fail about thirty years earlier, grew progressively worse, and he obtained an indult to recite by heart the Mass of the Blessed Virgin whenever his eyes were too weak to read the Mass of the day.

The last months of 1872, after he had finished the revision of the book of meditations, passed quietly. He was making plans for 1873, a Forty Hours devotion at the end of January and a retreat during the feast of Corpus Christi, but there were no immediate outside engagements. The days were spent in the solitude of his little room or in prayer in the chapel of the Marianites.

He was, however, always ready to help a friend. And when the pastor of a neighboring parish fell sick, he set off on the last day of the year to preach in his church on New Year's Day. During the night he experienced severe abdominal pains, but he got up in the morning and dragged himself to the church. He managed to preside at Mass and even to address a few words to the faithful. Then he let them take him back to Le Mans and call the doctor. He had celebrated the Holy Sacrifice for the last time.

For several days he insisted that there was nothing much the matter with him. He followed his usual routine, except that he was too weak to leave his room. Nor did he make any change in his meager diet, and he continued to sleep sitting in his armchair.

It was only after four days of illness that he yielded to the importunities of the doctor and Father Charles and agreed to be moved from his chair to a bed. The bed was in a bigger room, and he even agreed to a fire, a luxury he had not allowed for years. Once persuaded that he had to obey the doctor, he accepted whatever the doctor ordered. He had no human attachment left to anything, not even to his penitential practices. All he thought of was God, filling the day with prayer.

"As his illness increased, the soul of the venerable patient lifted itself to God by more continual aspirations," wrote Mother Mary of the Seven Dolors.

> He was praying constantly, and at any hour that he was approached during the day or during his prolonged periods of insomnia . . . he was heard reciting the invocations which his pious and retentive memory drew from the holy books or from the liturgy.

And still he looked forward to renewed activity in God's service, sending word to the pastor of Mont St. Jean that he hoped to be well enough to preach the Forty Hours on January 19. It was not to be. On January 17 he was given the Eucharist by Father Charles in the presence of the general council of the Marianites, and the following day he received the Sacrament of Anointing. It was clear to all that death was near, and two days later, January 20, Basil Moreau finally lay at peace. It was the moment for which his entire life had been a preparation, and he had approached it with serenity and confidence. "Thus dies the just man in the arms of his God," as he wrote in his meditation on death, "and his last sigh is the beginning of his glory and his new life."

Among his papers they found a spiritual testament dated June 13, 1867. It is an astonishing document, especially when one recalls that it was penned six months after its author's resignation as superior general and while he was still caught up in the intrigue and self-seeking which would continue until he was ousted from the work he had created. With more than human detachment from his surroundings, he struck a balance in terms of eternity. He proclaimed his filial obedience to the Holy See, asked pardon for unintentional offenses, thanked his relatives for understanding that he had not been ordained a priest to make them rich, and urged the priests, brothers, and sisters of Holy Cross to remain united in spirit and heart and in constant fidelity to the rules, even if separated in body.

Such were his thoughts, and, if there was one thing missing, it is supplied by what we might call a codicil drawn up four years later. After protesting that he never had regretted resigning as superior general, never had attempted to get the office back, never had a thought of not going to Rome once he was assured the Pope did not accept his excuses, never diverted funds of the Good Shepherd to Holy Cross, never diverted any public alms to his own family, he ended with the following characteristic declaration.

> I beg all the creditors of Notre-Dame de Sainte-Croix to be convinced that, at the time of my resignation as superior general, I left the Congregation with more than sufficient assets to pay off its debts and that I have never ceased to defend their interests.

> With all my heart I pardon and humbly beseech the Divine Mercy, through the intercession of the Blessed Virgin and St. Joseph, to pardon all those who have harmed my reputation or the goods I have held in trust, thanking God for having found me worthy to suffer something on the occasion of the undertakings, which I accepted for His glory.

CHAPTER FOURTEEN

The Cross Leads to the Crown

P roof of the solidity of the foundations on which Father Moreau had built is the fact that the edifice of Holy Cross survived the events related in the past several chapters. Survive it did, but, like its founder, it suffered and was humbled.

With the closing of the mother house, about thirty priests obtained dispensations from their vows and returned to diocesan work. Vocations dried up to the point where brothers were sent out in charge of schools with eight months, four months, or only fifteen days of novitiate. A few months after Father Moreau's death, the provincial for France, Father Rézé, wrote Father Sorin that the French clergy believed the Congregation had died in bankruptcy. Open a novitiate for the priests, he pleaded, even if we have to ask the Jesuits to lend us a novice master.

New tribulations were ahead, for the year of the founder's death was to go down in the Congregation's history as the year of the great liquidations. The mission to Bengal, after its toll of lives and money, was abandoned. The last schools in Algeria were closed. Cracow in Poland had been given up the previous year. Thirteen of the sixty houses which comprised the French province six years earlier had disappeared, and the attrition would continue until nothing would remain but the college at Neuilly, three large schools in La Mayenne, and about fifteen small village schools.

Father Sorin was not too concerned by all this decline. Although his residence as superior general was technically in France, he spent most of his time in the United States and concentrated his energies on the expansion of the Congregation in the New World. It was at this period that he wrote that Europe had become a domain claimed by wicked angels, perverse passions, spirits of darkness, and embassies of the Evil One, and he interpreted the decay of the French province as confirmation of his long-expressed conviction that the future of the Church and of Holy Cross lay in America.

Far from listening to the appeals of the provincial of France to send helpers from America, he neglected no opportunity to transfer a subject in the other direction. Even Father Hupier, despite his sixty-three years and poor health, was sent to Canada, where he died inside ten months, but not before establishing such a reputation for sanctity that the people among whom he had worked seized his body as it was being taken to the train and buried it lovingly in their own soil.

Events certainly confirmed Father Sorin's optimism regarding the role reserved for Holy Cross in America. Each year he saw his vision materialize. The number of students at Notre Dame reached five hundred by 1873, and the spirit that would continue to distinguish this center of education was already in evidence. Five years earlier, the graduates had formed the Alumni Association to strengthen that sense of pride in a Catholic elite, which was a major aim of Father Sorin's training.

Nearby St. Mary's Academy shared in Notre Dame's progress. Spacious buildings in beautiful surroundings were the external expression of a program, which won it a reputation as one of the country's top finishing schools for girls. By 1893, the sisters had a total of six academies and twelve schools, most of them in Indiana and Illinois.

In Canada, the growth of the Congregation followed a rhythm similar to that of the United States, if somewhat slower. St. Laurent College in Montreal got full teaching rights in 1860, and twenty years later it was affiliated with Laval University in Quebec. The sisters also expanded steadily and won a reputation for solid teaching in their many schools. They stayed under the jurisdiction of France when the Notre Dame branch separated in 1869, but they were forced by a new bishop to form a completely independent administration in 1882 under the name of Sisters of Holy Cross and the Seven Dolors (since 1981, Sisters of the Holy Cross). They had grown by 1961 to 169 houses, with 2,303 religious and a student enrollment of 59,174.

The celebration of Father Sorin's golden jubilee of ordination in 1888 made manifest the impact of his work on America. The spectacular demonstration at Notre Dame was presided over by Cardinal Gibbons, two archbishops, and twelve bishops. Representatives of the major groupings of clergy and laity joined in the tribute. Highlights of the ceremonies were the consecration of the new church and the laying of the foundation stone of Sorin Hall.

The following year, the Holy See gave evidence of a renewed confidence in Holy Cross. It entrusted to it again the Bengal mission lost in 1873. This time it was the American Province that would undertake the assignment.

Father Sorin was the last survivor of those who had played major roles in the formation and early struggles of Holy Cross. He died on October 31, 1893, twenty years after Father Moreau. From the day the grave had closed over him, he had never publicly referred to the founder nor taken any action to restore his memory. His last mention is found in the circular announcing Father Moreau's death and confirming the request for the suffrages prescribed for a superior general already made by the four members of the Congregation who had attended the funeral.

There is, nevertheless, at least one indication that he had not forgotten his former friend and superior. Father James Donahue, one of his successors as superior general of Holy Cross, has quoted him as having once remarked: "I was wrong! It was Father Moreau who was wise; we were only ignoramuses."

And what is certain is that the imprint of Father Moreau's method both as administrator and spiritual guide remained ever stamped on his successor. The devotions dearest to the founder were those he sought to revive and expand in the Congregation. In 1873, he consecrated the new ecclesiastical province of Cincinnati to the Sacred Heart. St. Joseph he held up constantly in his circular letters as a guide and inspiration to all the religious, especially the brothers. Most characteristic of all was his devotion to our Lady, in whose honor he established the *Ave Maria* magazine in 1865.

His exhortations on observance of the rules echoed the very words of Father Moreau, an ironic echo in view of his own reaction when they were addressed to him. "I absolutely forbid any of our houses to incur any expenses beyond the approved budget. . . . The man who contracts debts is soon regarded as an object of universal contempt." Earlier he used to complain that Father Moreau was quick to invoke the vow of obedience to reinforce his orders. Now he himself was more forthright. Violators of his prescriptions would be excluded from the sacraments. He was a strange man, a man of extremes, a man hard to capture. And, yet, his immense contributions to the expansion of the Catholic Church in the United States, as well as to that of the Congregation of Holy Cross, his personal piety, his dedicated life, his edifying death, all confirmed the basic correctness of Father Moreau's judgment in choosing him to be his chief lieutenant.

Father Gilbert Français was named coadjutor to Father Sorin a year before his death, and he succeeded him as superior general. He re-established the generalate in France and began recruitment on a scale unknown there since Father Moreau's time. Soon he had thirty novices in an excellently organized novitiate near Angers and houses of studies for both clerics and brothers. His main helper was a Father Lemarié, provincial for France, who had been a close associate of Father Moreau and had always remained faithful to him. He had actually left the Congregation under pressure after Father Moreau had resigned as superior general, but had returned in 1887 when the atmosphere was more peaceful.

Father Lemarié was the first person of standing within the Congregation to attempt the rehabilitation of the founder, beginning with the commissioning of a portrait based on the only photograph ever taken of Father Moreau. Father Français supported his efforts, even initiating plans to write a biography. In 1899, he commemorated the centenary of the founder's birth with a circular letter and the distribution of a pamphlet written by a grandnephew of Father Moreau.

The laws against religious associations promulgated in France in 1901 and 1904 wiped out almost the entire reflowering of Holy Cross. The houses and schools were turned over to the diocesan clergy or expropriated. A few priests clung on, as did a few brothers who continued to teach but without wearing their habit. Father Français moved the generalate once more to Notre Dame, Indiana, where it remained until 1941. After brief periods in Washington, D. C., and New York, it was established in Rome in 1954. There it continues to guide the progress of the priests and the brothers. Between them, they were providing the kind of education which was a major motive of Father Moreau's in founding the Congregation to students in higher, secondary, and elementary education in France, the United States, Canada, Brazil, Chile, Peru, Haiti, Ghana, Uganda, India, and Bangladesh.

Father Français was succeeded in 1926 by Father James Donahue, a man whose previous work had been characterized by deep understanding of the spiritual life, as retreat preacher, novice master, and superior of houses of studies at Notre Dame and Rome. That same year he was visited at Notre Dame by Bishop Grente of Le Mans. Bishop Grente, later Archbishop, Cardinal, and member of the French Academy, had long shown a friendly interest in the founder of Holy Cross and had worked with the members of the French province and with the Marianites of Le Mans to glorify him. The upshot of his visit was an invitation to Holy Cross to reopen a house at Le Mans after a lapse of sixty-five years.

The mother church was still standing, although in a very dilapidated condition. The army had used it as a warehouse. In 1931, the Congregation was able to buy it back, together with an adjoining house built by the Jesuits. Restoration began immediately, and the church was reconsecrated in 1937 in the presence of the superior general, the entire council of priests and brothers, and religious of all three branches of the sisters. On this occasion, in a reference to Father Moreau and his work, the superior general, Father Donahue, declared, "We are today assisting at the triumph of truth and sanctity." The remark was characteristic of Father Donahue, for there is not one of his circular letters to the Congregation which does not preach enthusiastically the duty to return wholeheartedly to the spirit of the founder.

Like the priests and brothers, the Marianite Sisters had nearly all been driven into exile from France in the first years of the twentieth century. Taking refuge in the United States, they helped to expand the work of the houses in New York and Louisiana. After World War I, they began once more to build up schools, hospitals, and other activities in France; and after World War II, they had the satisfaction of returning also to Bengladesh. Marianite houses in 1961 numbered 65, with 630 religious and 21,622 students. They conduct one liberal arts college, eleven secondary and forty-one primary schools, thirteen hospitals, a sanatorium, and a leprosarium. The houses are located in France (where the mother house is again at Le Mans), Pakistan, Haiti, and Canada and in the United States in New York, New Jersey, and Louisiana.

The French-Canadian Father Albert Cousineau, who followed Father Donahue as superior general in 1938, continued where he left off. When Father Moreau's remains were transferred to the crypt of the mother church in November 1938, he formalized the Congregation's reparation of the memory of its founder.

"As the fifth successor of Very Reverend Father Moreau," he said,

> I wish to declare before these sacred remains that
> we, his children—priests, brothers, sisters—recog-
> nize him as our worthy founder who, having been
> humiliated and cruelly tried by unjust treatment, has
> given fruitfulness to the Congregation of Holy Cross
> through his tears and sacrifices. We ask his pardon
> for all the injustice, abandonment, and perhaps trea-
> son which he had to suffer at our hands.

A logical next step, doubly appropriate in Father Moreau's case, was to ask Rome to declare officially the holiness of the founder of the Congregation of Holy Cross. Once again, the first step was the privilege of the bishop of Le Mans, but this time there was no problem obtaining his cooperation. In 1946, Father Cousineau and the superiors general of the three branches of Holy Cross sisters met at Le Mans and laid their request before Bishop Grente, who forthwith submitted his own petition to the Holy See to obtain introduction of the Cause of Beatification of Father Moreau.

A diocesan tribunal to organize the Cause of Beatification was created at Le Mans the following year, and the Holy See designat-ed Monsignor René Fontenelle as Postulator of the Cause. It was a moment of great joy for the nearly eighteen hundred religious who were members of the Congregation of Holy Cross and the more than twenty thousand students then enrolled in the schools throughout the world.

A canonization process is normally a protracted undertak-ing. The first step is to assemble for examination the writings of the Servant of God (to use the traditional title accorded to one judged worthy to be subjected to the scrutiny of his words and acts, which is the prelude to canonization).

Father Moreau's writings are extremely extensive. He pub-lished scores of books and booklets on a great variety of devo-tional subjects. His circular letters to his religious fill two big volumes. His correspondence with individuals was abundant. The collection and study of them all took several years, but finally in 1952 the Sacred Congregation of Rites was able to announce that the work was completed and that it gave its official approval to the writings of Father Moreau. A major step had been taken.

Simultaneously, the testimony was taken of twenty-one witnesses who were in a position to speak from their firsthand knowledge of Father Moreau or of others who figured importantly in his life. One of these, a grandniece of the Abbot of Solesmes, Dom Guéranger, had this to say in the course of her presentation:

> I saw him (on one occasion) on a sidewalk a few steps away from the college gate, surrounded by seven or eight persons. My companion said: 'That's Father Moreau.' I looked attentively at him. I had heard a lot about him, and I was glad to see him. The clear recollection I retain is specifically that I was struck by his appearance which reflected an intense interior life, a deep humility and a charity without limits. I have never heard anything about him that was not wholly favorable. I am sure that if Dom Guéranger had any other kind of views on Father Moreau, I could not have escaped hearing them in my family. I know that he had extreme difficulties, first in the financial and subsequently in the moral order, and that he bore them with astonishing patience, as the saints do.
>
> That is what people round me said. That was my family's understanding. I know that he lived in extreme poverty in a small house near the college. His poverty and humility were extraordinary. I know that Father Moreau had to suffer greatly, and that his acceptance of these sufferings was heroic.

When the diocesan tribunal had completed its informative process at Le Mans, the documents for the Cause were submitted to Rome. After discussion at the Sacred Congregation of Rites, a plenary meeting of the cardinals of the Sacred Congregation on May 12, 1955, officially introduced the Cause and took it under the authority of the Holy See. Two months later, Cardinal Grente of Le Mans officially opened the Apostolic Process, and the work of this phase of the Cause continued until the spring of 1957, when the entire file of the process was delivered to the Sacred Congregation of Rites.

The next step was the official copying and the preparation of the legal brief to establish the heroic practice by Father Moreau of the theological and cardinal virtues. The brief took several years to complete, but finally it was submitted to the Promoter General of the Faith (popularly known as the devil's advocate) on May 10, 1961. The task of the Promoter is to formulate objections and criticisms to which the Postulator responds. The Congregation of Rites discusses the case and makes a recommendation to the Pope. Following a favorable recommendation, the Holy Father decrees that the Servant of God practiced virtue in a heroic degree, and so declares the person "Venerable."[3]

A part of Father Moreau's life that was investigated closely involved his difficulties with the Sacred Congregation of Propaganda. This, however, did not create a new problem for the Congregation of Rites. Cardinal Barnabo himself foresaw the possibility. "Remember what they did to St. Joseph Calasanctius," he said jokingly to Father Moreau one day in September 1868, at the height of their differences. "They dragged him in a cart across Rome to the Holy Office, and later they beatified him."

St. Philip Neri, no less ardent a devotee of the Holy See than Father Moreau, suffered a like experience. He was accused of trying to foment a heretical sect and brought before the Inquisition. His worst persecutor was a pope who himself was also canonized, Pius V. St. Alphonsus Liguori was deposed by the Holy See from his office of superior general and was later expelled from the Congregation he had founded.

Such misjudgments are common with all great people, for their genuine worth and rightful place in history are usually established only years after their death. The founders and found-resses of religious institutes seem to be selected by providence to illustrate this law in a special way. And harsh as the experience is, it would seem in the designs of providence to fulfill a double purpose, to ensure their personal sanctification by despoiling them of what they inevitably prize most highly in the world, and to ensure the full establishment of their work by launching it on the independent course for which it is designed. It is indeed the fulfillment of the law of nature and of grace which Christ proclaimed when He declared that the seed must fall in the earth and die before it can produce its fruit.

A RARE MAN
SELECTED BY PROVIDENCE

Afterword
by
Joel Giallanza, C.S.C.

Gary MacEoin opens his biography of the founder of the Holy Cross family with a marvelous insight, "Basil Anthony Mary Moreau was one of the rare men who alter the course of history." This simple statement has been confirmed over the years that have passed since Father Moreau's life and death in the nineteenth century. That confirmation is evident especially in the several decades since the appearance of MacEoin's work in the mid-twentieth century. Today we have an enhanced awareness of the rich and living legacy that Basil Moreau passed on, not only to the religious of Holy Cross and those who minister with them, but to all who are committed to continuing the mission and message of Jesus.

That awareness did not come quickly. After the life of a founder or foundress of a religious community, the usual course of events involves an exploration and elaboration of the example and teaching of that founding person so future generations can adopt and adapt the basic principles for life and ministry that reflect the gifts with which God blessed the person. Such a course did not unfold after Father Moreau's death. There was, in fact, a silence that shrouded his memory among the members of Holy Cross, except for the Marianite Sisters whose fidelity never wavered. That silence spanned more than five decades. As MacEoin notes, there were internal difficulties, disputes, and divisions among the members of Holy Cross before Father Moreau's resignation and after his death. This turbulent atmosphere, in addition to the, at times, careless disposal of Moreau's personal effects, hindered the collection, preservation, and translation of primary materials by and about him. And many who knew and worked personally with Father Moreau lived the remainder of their days in that silence, thus taking with them the possibility of developing an authentic oral tradition about the personality and perspectives of the founder that no documentary sources could capture completely. The consequences of those silent years are still encountered today by those who undertake scholarly work with the sources available on Basil Moreau.

Gradually, through the study, research, and writing of several brothers, sisters, and priests after the first decades of the twentieth century, the members of Holy Cross were reintroduced to Moreau's life, work, and teaching. In recent years this expanded to include reflections on the significance of Basil Moreau's accomplishments for today's world, society, and church. Through the efforts of those who continue to study and research Moreau sources, and with the increase of materials available for distribution, the Family of Holy Cross, as well as those associated with it by ministry and friendship, are embracing anew the words and wisdom that the founder brings into their lives.

Like Father Moreau's life, the heritage that flows from his example and teaching is complex. In his presentation of this holy man, which was gleaned from the much more comprehensive 1955 biography by Etienne and Tony Catta, Gary MacEoin touches on that complexity from a historical and biographical perspective. Because Holy Cross does not have a reliable oral tradition that can trace its roots to Moreau's contemporaries, that perspective is particularly important. The research and reflection that continues today can benefit from that perspective, enlarge it, and so amplify the information we have about Father Moreau and sharpen our appreciation of his contribution to the times in which we live. These present reflections will highlight some of the principal areas being focused on in that research and reflection.

"Promoting the Kingdom of God"

MacEoin's biography presents Basil Moreau as a man of God, a man committed to doing God's will, a man in love with God. The founder of Holy Cross, the author notes, "not only became a priest and a religious but dedicated all his energies throughout his life to the single purpose of promoting the Kingdom of God." This dedication marks Moreau's life, for all of his life, and he wanted it to mark the lives of Holy Cross religious. In recent years there has been an increased attention given to Moreau's perspective on the key elements for building and maintaining a relationship with God. This has been and continues to be challenging because the founder did not articulate a systematic approach to the spiritual life. Though he began to move in that direction during the 1840s, he abandoned the project to focus on the persons of Jesus, Mary, and Joseph in lieu of distinctive devotions for his religious family. In guiding the men and women of Holy Cross, Father Moreau drew upon the wealth and wisdom of several mystical traditions with which he was familiar: Sulpician, Ignatian, Benedictine, Salesian, Carmelite, and the French School.

Primary among the elements of his spirituality is the indispensability of imitating Jesus and continuing his mission. The supporting components that he proposed for this imitation and continuation are simple and straightforward. Moreau lived with, and insisted on the need for, a keen sense of trust in divine providence—that is, the conviction that God is present and active regardless of the situation and our experience of it. That conviction is nurtured by fidelity to personal and communal prayer and is supported by a community life that is loving, reconciling, genuinely concerned for one another, and hospitable to everyone. All this is expressed through commitment to the religious vows and to the transformation they facilitate. Father Moreau knew, by faith and experience, that such a life, inevitably, would encounter the cross. That encounter and our response to it will define the caliber of our spiritual lives. For this reason, Basil Moreau situates the Family of Holy Cross, within the Paschal Mystery, at the foot of the cross next to Mary of Sorrows, Our Lady of Holy Cross. From there, as pure gift, comes the grace of new life.

Father Moreau tells us, "Christianity—and with still great reason the religious life—is nothing else than the life of Jesus Christ reproduced in our conduct" (*Circular Letter* 137). The quality of our life for the future will be gauged by our willingness to explore as fully as possible what this means, concretely, for the world in which we live. Basil Moreau was a man of God. His life and legacy are pathways for us to become people of God.

"Less Interested in Theory Than in Action"

As Gary MacEoin portrays him, Moreau was a man of vision. He could see what needed to be done, then he would organize and mobilize the resources necessary to do it. Part of this characterizes his personality, and part marks the age in which he lived. As the biographer observes, "Father Moreau and his contemporaries were less interested in theory than in action. They belonged to a generation which thought it had all the answers." This trait served the founder well as the Family of Holy Cross began to develop and move beyond the borders of France. He had the ability to see the potential that could be tapped by uniting the few

Auxiliary Priests and a small community known as the Brothers of Saint Joseph. And, as the author points out, "with the establishment of the sisters, the Congregation had assumed its definitive form."

Studies in recent years uncovered some historical insights to which MacEoin did not have complete access. First, with a deeper understanding of the plan envisioned by Father Jacques Dujarié in founding the Sisters of Divine Providence and the Brothers of Saint Joseph, we can recognize now Moreau's respect for and attentiveness to all that Dujarié had accomplished. At the same time, he was creative and insightful in building from and expanding upon those accomplishments. Second, the life of the first brothers has come more sharply into focus. And, as MacEoin says, "the spirituality and dedication of Brother André were to serve the group well." It is clear that the brothers were concerned about the quality of their service, their efforts to remain in contact with Father Dujarié and one another, and their involvement in the lives of the people. Third, we know more about the first ministries in which the sisters were involved. Though domestic services occupied a large part of their workday, they had the apostolic energy, creativity, and sensitivity to provide day care as well as basic lessons in catechetics and home economics to girls and women who needed assistance. Finally, and unfortunately, not much additional information has come to light regarding the Auxiliary Priests. It is known that Father Moreau composed a rule of life for them, which they adopted; however, there is no text extant. Because the priests, as an independent group, were in existence for such a brief time before becoming a part of Holy Cross, there may not be much more that can be known about them.

In articulating his vision, Father Moreau wrote that his plan "was to found three establishments consecrated to the Most Holy Hearts of Jesus, Mary, and Joseph; although living in separate dwellings and under different rules would, nevertheless, remain united among themselves after the model of the Holy Family"

(*Circular Letter* 8). That vision enabled Holy Cross religious to live and minister around the world while striving to remain close to one another and to the people they serve. The challenge is to assure that those efforts remain fresh so they can be a witness to all people that unity in the midst of diversity is truly a possibility. Basil Moreau was a man of vision. Our daily life is the means through which the vision will become action for the good of society and the church. Our work and our witness will demonstrate that we, too, are people of vision.

"Modern and Practical Approach"

This biography also introduces us to a man of mission. Father Moreau was passionate in his desire to respond to people's needs to the best of his ability; he was known for his zeal. This was true for all his ministerial interests, especially those in which he envisioned Holy Cross religious involved: education, parish ministry, and the foreign missions. This was the case especially for his commitment to education. MacEoin tells us, "He had a modern and practical approach to the content of education, always insisting that education was intended to prepare for living, and that the vast majority of the students were going to live in the world." Father Moreau believed that students should experience continuity between what they learned and experienced in school and what they would do and experience once they had families and entered the business world. They were to be prepared for everyday life. This modern and practical approach was to become the hallmark of Holy Cross education.

Considerable research and reflection has been done in recent years regarding Moreau's philosophy of education. Though MacEoin does recognize some ways in which the founder was a pioneer in this field, the extent to which Father Moreau was a genuine innovator has become even clearer since this volume's original publication. He understood that the entire person needed to be engaged in the educational process if the experiences and

learning in school were to have any lasting influence and significance in shaping the person's life. "We shall always place education side by side with instruction; the mind will not be cultivated
at the expense of the heart. While we prepare useful citizens for
society, we shall likewise do our utmost to prepare citizens for
eternal life" (*Circular Letter* 36). This seminal statement from the
founder has stimulated both personal and institutional discussion
and reflection on the Holy Cross character of the school and of
the education provided. Basil Moreau's philosophy of education
constitutes a process that is designed to serve students long after
their years in school. The information communicated to them
must be more than mere data; it should be presented in such a
way that it becomes an integral part of their academic, personal,
social, and spiritual formation. This formation will transmit the
values by which students make decisions and take directions; it
will influence their quality of life for the future. As it deepens,
such a formation, and their service to others, will engage them
in the transformation of the society in which they live and work.
The interaction and integration of these three—information,
formation, transformation—compel Father Moreau to describe
education as "this work of resurrection" (*Christian Education*).

The founder's apostolic mandate to the Family of Holy Cross
is clear: "We are committed by our vocation to extend the reign
of Jesus Christ in the hearts of all people" (*Exercises*). The challenge is to fulfill that mandate in whichever circumstances our
vocation places us and through whichever ministry we serve others, for the mission and message of Jesus have value for every circumstance and in every age. Basil Moreau was a man of mission.
Our service to others will have a transformative effect insofar as
we are committed to being people of mission.

"Get People to Come Together"

Gary MacEoin recognizes that Basil Moreau was a man
involved in many relationships, familial and personal, ecclesiastical

and political, social and formal. This spectrum of relationships is a testimony to the truth that Father Moreau was a man of love. His ability to relate to others and to express care and compassion for them stood as an invitation for them to share in and even promote his projects. As the biographer indicates, "Basil Moreau's genius was that he could get people to come together and pool their efforts to accomplish the purposes he proposed." It is not surprising that one of his favorite images for Holy Cross is the family. The founder knew that he could not realize his dreams alone. He needed others and appreciated that truth of his humanity throughout his almost seventy-four years of life.

When there is no extensive oral tradition surrounding the founder of a religious community, whatever visuals are available become quite important. In Father Moreau's case, there is but one photograph, taken in 1856 at a time when he was not well, affected by a cataract, and not pleased with the plot used to make the photograph possible. His unhappy visage, combined with the stories of his austerities and penitential practices, gave rise to an image of the man as stern, aloof, austere, unsmiling, unaffected, and unaffectionate. That image prevailed for several decades after his death. As his writings and especially his personal letters were studied, a different image began to take shape. Though he is clearly a man of uncompromising integrity with a keen sense of justice, his correspondence reveals a person who knew and enjoyed many people. In his exchanges, he would challenge and cajole, explain and excuse, invite and invoke, forewarn and forgive. His words are those of a warm man who made friends and acquaintances from all sectors of church and society. He knew well the men and women of Holy Cross, personally at first, and then through letters as the community expanded numerically and geographically. Moreau insisted that the members of Holy Cross "have great respect, sincere esteem, and cordial affection for each other, living together as friends strictly united" (*Rules*). These are words from a man of love; he strived to be that in all his relationships.

Father Moreau had the ability to bring together very diverse people for a common project primarily because he would appeal to the heart. He would speak of the need for and wisdom of interdependence, teaching that "the activity of the individual will help the community, and the activity of the community will, in turn, help each individual. (*Circular Letter* 65). The challenge for today is to demonstrate that such interdependence is possible in our world and work and neighborhood. Basil Moreau was a man of love. We know this is the way, for we know that love sums up the example of Jesus. It remains for us to follow that way and live that example and so become people of love.

"Selected by Providence"

The world has changed. The times in which we live may have more parallels to Moreau's own times than when Gary MacEoin's biography first appeared. Nineteenth-century France was familiar with social turmoil, economic inequities, mistrust of government officials, doubts about the church, international wars, concerns and fears for the future. Similar themes are echoed for us today in the morning newspaper and in the evening news reports. In such a context Basil Moreau was called by God to revitalize faith and to rebuild society. This revitalization and rebuilding are principal elements of the charism that has become his lasting legacy to the Family of Holy Cross and to the whole church.

Father Moreau knew that there would be a personal price to pay; after all, in response to the call he received, he chose to live the message and example of Jesus. He knew there would be more than one death to self to be experienced if he was to become and be a man of God, vision, mission, and love. He learned what it meant to encounter and embrace the cross. There were many; crosses came both from within and without the Holy Cross family. But such is God's work. As MacEoin wisely observes, "The founders of religious institutes seem to be selected by providence to illustrate this law in a special way." Truly, Basil Moreau was a man selected by providence.

Gary MacEoin opens his biography by describing the founder of Holy Cross as a man who altered history. He concludes his work by referring to Jesus' teaching in John 12:24:"the seed must fall in the earth and die before it can produce its fruit." Father Moreau's experience has produced much fruit that will shape the future. The seed sown by his life and example continues to be creative and productive. There is much yet to be explored and expressed from the rich heritage given to us by Basil Moreau. Within his words and wisdom and way of life there is a spirituality for all people. There are more implications to be gleaned from his life's work and teaching that will be of benefit to those serving others through education, social justice, and parish ministry—indeed, through all forms of service anywhere in the world. The evolution of the Holy Cross charism can be further elaborated regarding interdependence in ministry as laity and ordained, women and men. There are finer points to be articulated from Basil Moreau's teaching regarding the responsibilities to which God calls us and the transformation that God promises to each of us.

That promise and the transformation accompanying it are, essentially, apostolic; their effects will extend far beyond the individual. Father Moreau tells educators that, through their ministry, "you will contribute to preparing the world for better times than ours" (*Christian Education*). Whatever our vocation, whatever our work, this is a contribution to which all of us must be fully committed. Such a commitment will be a means for us to bring a resounding message of hope to our world. This was a matter of urgency for Basil Moreau, and so it must be for us.

Bibliography

Catta, Etienne, and Tony Catta, *Basil Anthony Mary Moreau* (Milwaukee: The Bruce Publishing Company, 1955).

Moreau, Basile, *Circular Letters*, Translated and Edited by Joel Giallanza, C.S.C. and Jacques Grisé, C.S.C. (Rome: Congregation of Holy Cross, 1998).

———, *Constitutions and Rules* (Le Mans: Congregation of Holy Cross, 1858).

———, *Pédagogie chrétienne* (Le Mans: Julien Printing Shop, 1856). Translated as *Christian Education* by various editors.

Chronology

July 14, 1789 ....After years of financial struggle and volatile class relations, the French Revolution begins with the storming of the Bastille prison.

February 13, 1790 ....The National Assembly prohibits monastic vows and abolishes all religious orders, except those dedicated to teaching and charity.

November 27, 1790 ....Priests throughout France are required to sign an oath of loyalty to the new French nation.

February 11, 1799 ....Basil Anthony Mary Moreau is born in the French village Laigné-en-Belin.

July 15, 1801 ....Concordant between Rome and the Emperor Napoleon, restoring Roman Catholicism in France.

1814....................................Basil Moreau begins high school and then matriculates to St. Vincent's, the diocesan seminary at Chateau-Gontier.

July 15, 1820 ....Father Jacques Dujarié founds the Brothers of St. Joseph

August 12, 1821 ....Moreau is ordained a priest at the Visitation convent in Le Mans, France.

1821–1823...........................Father Moreau spends two years studying at the seminary St. Sulpice in Paris where he encounters Father Gabriel Mollevaut who serves as his spiritual director for twenty-five years.

May 26, 1825......................Father Moreau appointed professor of Dogmatic Theology at St. Vincent's Seminary, Le Mans.

1833....................................Moreau oversees the establishment of the Association of the Good Shepherd, a religious community of Sisters for whom Moreau would be superior until 1858.

243

August 31, 1835 ....Father Jacques Dujarié resigns as leader of the Brothers of St. Joseph; Moreau is appointed as the new superior.

1835....................................Father Moreau founds the Auxiliary Priests.

March 1, 1837 ....The Brothers of St. Joseph and the Auxiliary Priests unite to form the Association of Holy Cross, a major step toward the formal creation of the family of Holy Cross.

April 28, 1840 ....First mission to Algeria sets off.

August 15, 1840 ....Moreau and four other priests profess vows as religious.

1840....................................Holy Cross sisters founded, known as the Marianites of Holy Cross.

August 5, 1841 ....Seven Holy Cross religious depart Le Mans to begin a mission in the United States: Father Edward Sorin; Brothers Vincent, Joachim, Lawrence, Mary, Gatien, and Anselm.

April 1852...........................The Sacred Congregation for the Propagation of the Faith begins reviewing the affairs of Holy Cross.

May 13, 1857 ....Pope Pius IX approves the constitutions of Holy Cross but separates the Marianites to develop as an independent congregation.

1860–1866 ....Period of financial and institutional struggle for Holy Cross, especially for Father Moreau.

August 1863 ....General chapter authorizes the creation of both a French and North American Province for the Congregation. French province established.

May 1865 ....North American Province established at Notre Dame, Indiana.

June 10, 1866 ....Pope Pius IX accepts Father Moreau's resignation as superior general of Holy Cross.

February 19, 1867 ....Constitutions and Rule of the Mariantes first approved by the Bishop of Le Mans.

July 1869 ....Marianites in the United States become an independent religious congregation known as the Sisters of the Holy Cross.

January 20, 1873 ....Father Basil Moreau dies at age seventy-three.

January 1883 ....Marianites in Canada become an independent religious congregation known as the Sisters of Holy Cross and of the Seven Dolors.

1955 ....The Cause of Father Moreau formally opens.

July 21, 1955 ....Moreau declared "Servant of God," the first of four stages toward canonization.

May 1961............................The Promoter of the Faith for the Cause of Father Moreau submits to the Vatican Congregation of Rites the required supporting documents testifying to Father Moreau's heroic virtues, which are necessary for declaring him "Venerable."

October 1962......................Pope John XXIII convenes the Second Vatican Council, postponing the Cause toward Moreau's canonization.

April 12, 2003 ....Father Moreau is declared "Venerable" by Pope John Paul II.

April 2006 ....Pope Benedict XVI promulgates an authorized miracle attributed to the intercession of Father Moreau, thus ensuring his beatification.

Index

About the Author

One the most prolific and influential Catholic journalists of the twentieth century, Gary MacEoin was the author of twenty-five books, including *The People's Church: Bishop Samuel Ruiz of Mexico and Why He Matters*, as well as the editor of *The Papacy and the People of God*. During his seventy-year career, MacEoin was an accomplished editor, speechwriter, public relations spokesman, union representative, and most importantly, champion for social justice. MacEoin had a long-standing relationship with the *National Catholic Reporter* dating from the paper's beginnings in the 1960s. He died in 2003 at the age of ninety-four.

Brother Joel Giallanza, C.S.C., is a member of the South-West Province of Brothers of the Congregation of Holy Cross and is the author of *Source and Summit: Six Great Spiritual Guides Talk About the Eucharist* and *Questions Jesus Asked: Provisions for the Spiritual Journey*. Brother Joel revised and updated the text of this new edition of Gary MacEoin's biography of Father Moreau.

With nearly 2,000 priests, brothers, sisters, and seminarians in universities, colleges, high schools, foreign missions, parishes, social justice ministries, and other apostolic works on five continents, Holy Cross is growing in the twenty-first century as Educators in the Faith. The community's seal is the cross and anchors with the motto, "Ave Crux Spes Unica," The Cross, Our Only Hope. Its initials (C.S.C.) are Latin for Congregatio a Santa Cruce.

CONGREGATION OF
HOLY CROSS
EDUCATION · PARISH · MISSION

vocation.nd.edu

As we grow in age, we grow in love for prayer.
Oh! Let us pray more than ever, and spread around us, by example and teaching,
by constant and increasing efforts, the wholesome, the saving spirit of prayer.
—Edward Sorin, C.S.C.

The Cross, Our Only Hope
Daily Reflections in the Holy Cross Tradition
Edited by Andrew Gawrych, C.S.C., and Kevin Grove, C.S.C.
Members of the Congregation of Holy Cross—including pastors, teachers, and the current and past presidents of the University of Notre Dame—offer an introduction to the rich, vibrant spirituality of the Congregation through a series of daily meditations on the themes of the Holy Cross spiritual tradition, including trust in God, compassion, hope in the cross, discipleship, and the promotion of justice.
ISBN: 9781594711626 / 416 pages / $15.95

Available from your bookstore or from
ave maria press / Notre Dame, IN 46556
www.avemariapress.com / Ph: 800-282-1865
ave maria press®   A Ministry of the Indiana Province of Holy Cross

Keycode: F0A0807000000